Everyday Literacies in Africa
Ethnographic Studies of Literacy and Numeracy Practices in Ethiopia

Alemayehu Hailu Gebre
Alan Rogers
Brian Street
George Openjuru

FOUNTAIN PUBLISHERS
Kampala

Fountain Publishers Ltd
P. O. Box 488 Kampala
E-mail: sales@fountainpublishers.co.ug
         publishing@ fountainpublishers.co.ug
Website:www.fountainpublishers.co.ug

Distributed in Europe and Commonwealth
countries outside Africa by:
African Books Collective,
P.O. Box 721, Oxford OX1 9EN, UK.
Tel: 44(0) 1869 349110, Fax:+44(0)1869 349110
E-mail: orders@africanbookscollective.com
Website: www.africanbookscollective.com

© A.H. Gebre, A. Rogers, B. Street & G. Openjuru 2009
First published 2009

All rights reserved. No part of this publication may be reproduced, stored in a retrieval system or transmitted in any form or by any means electronic, mechanical, photocopying, recording or otherwise without the prior written permission of the publisher.

ISBN 978-9970-02-975-4

Contents

PART I: ETHNOGRAPHIC APPROACHES TO LITERACY AND NUMERACY

1. **Ethnographic Approaches to Literacy and Numeracy** — 1
   - "Starting where they are" — 1
   - Finding out: The traditional approach — 2
   - Informal learning and tacit funds of knowledge — 3
   - What do we mean by an ethnographic approach? — 5
   - Ethnography as a window on literacy and numeracy — 15
   - How do we use ethnographic approaches – tools and methods — 19

2. **Literacy and Numeracy in Livelihoods** — 39
   - Case Study 1A: Women in Small Scale Business in Arbaminch Town — 39
   - Case Study 1B: A Co-operative Business: Hambelle and Guye — 41
   - Case Study 1C: Guyato, a trader of Konsosefer — 44
   - Case Study 2: Tirhas: A small scale business in Adwa, Tigray — 49
   - Case Study 3: Literacy and Numeracy in Life's Histories – Small Scale Industry — 54
   - Case Study 4: Literacy and Numeracy in the Marketplace — 59
   - Case Study 5: Three Traders in Aleltu Market in Cheese and Butter, Meat and Grain — 61
   - Case Study 6: Abate the Butcher Muddles through Life with Multiple Skills — 72
   - Case Study 7: Enani, a farmer in the market — 75
   - Case Study 8: Literacy and Numeracy in Life Histories — 86
   - Case Study 9: Almaz: A Story of a Young Illiterate Woman who Won a Court Case — 88
   - Case Study 10: Literacy and Numeracy in Rural Lives — 92
   - Case Study 11: A Farming Family — 111

PART II: SOME FINDINGS FROM THE CASE STUDIES AND THEIR IMPLICATIONS FOR TEACHING LITERACY AND NUMERACY TO ADULTS

3. Teaching Literacy and Numeracy to Adults — 118
   Some conclusions — 118
   Other findings from our case studies and fieldwork — 126
   Focusing on the daily lives as a whole — 126
   Implications for adult literacy learning programmes — 132
   A new approach to adult learners — 133
   The Nirantar model — 135
   Using the findings in the adult classroom — 140
   The CRB approach — 140
   Some learning themes from the case studies — 143
   Four examples of developing learning programmes from ethnographic findings — 145
   Counting — 146
   Measuring — 147
   Income and expenditure — 147
   Proverbs, songs and poems — 149
   Conclusion — 150
   References and further reading — 151

PART I

Ethnographic Approaches to
Literacy and Numeracy

1
Ethnographic Approaches to Literacy and Numeracy

This book outlines the story of a journey – a journey towards a clearer and more focused understanding of what literacy and numeracy mean in the context of rural and urban society in a country like Ethiopia. The starting point for this journey was the desire of a group of practitioners in Ethiopia to build more effective learning programmes for adults who wish to develop their literacy and numeracy skills and practices, whether through designing better learning programmes, preparing more relevant teaching-learning materials or training literacy instructors.

"Starting where they are"

Virtually every manual for the training of adult literacy instructors or facilitators contains a section on adult learning. It goes something like this: "ADULT LEARNING: Adults learn differently from children. Adults bring to their learning a great deal of experience and existing knowledge. Facilitators must build on this experience and knowledge. 'Start where they are'"

During the third LETTER workshop in Debre Zeit in April-May 2008, we examined about a dozen such literacy manuals from Ethiopia, and found they all contained some such training session. One of the manuals we examined put it like this:

> "Adults are not like children who are expected to take everything that they are told by a trainer. So training should take into consideration that adults do have rich experience to the extent of participating in social activities and may have richer experiences than the trainer may have."

Many other kinds of adult learning programmes follow this approach. Agricultural extension workers, for example, are almost always aware that the men and women they are dealing with are already farming and seek to build on these practices. Much (but not all) health extension, especially in nutrition programmes, start by examining with the learners their existing practices, beliefs and remedies – for example, what their practices of food selection, marketing and cooking are. They seek out and build on local knowledge.

Traditionally, however, adult literacy and numeracy are treated differently. The world is divided into two, the literate and the illiterate; and by definition, it is thought that illiterates know nothing about and have no experience of literacy. In this case, the adult learners (so it is assumed) do not bring any existing experience and knowledge with them. It is taken for granted that 'starting where they are' means starting without any perception of what literacy and numeracy mean, without any existing skills or practices.

And many adult 'illiterates' have internalised this themselves. They too claim that they are illiterate, ignorant, indeed (as one of our informants said) 'a non-person'; that they have nothing to bring to their literacy/numeracy learning.

But this does not tally with life. We know that all adults (including so-called 'illiterates') can and do count, that they can and do measure and calculate (for example, in the market, in cooking or in farming) – in other words, they engage in numeracy activities. We know that they can and do negotiate literacy tasks such as money, bills, letters, election notices etc. And in any case, so-called 'illiterates' have experience, often deep experience, of being excluded from literacy activities – they see texts and many think, 'That is not for me'.

So adults do bring to adult literacy learning programmes experience and knowledge, perceptions and some practices relating to both literacy and numeracy. So, if the facilitator is to 'start where they are', is to build on their existing knowledge and experience, how can we and the facilitators find out what they know and do?

That was the core question we set ourselves. This formed the basis of the training programme in the three LETTER workshops and in the exercises undertaken between each of the workshops. This is the journey we began in September 2007; and this is what is described in this book.

Finding out: The traditional approach

Now, the simple way would be simply to ask them what their experience of literacy and numeracy has been. That is certainly a good starting point. But we would argue that it is not, by itself, good enough – for three main reasons:

First, a great deal of experience of questionnaire surveys like market research reveals that people tell the questioner what the respondent feels the questioner wants to know. We call this the 'echo effect' – people echo back to the researcher what they know is in the mind of the researcher. They tend to talk about those things which they know are important to the researcher rather than what is important to them.

For (and this is the second reason), they may feel that what they know and what they practise is not important, at least not important enough to mention to the researcher. In their view, what they do in the way of literacy and numeracy 'doesn't count' because it has not been learned in school.

But much more important than these two, they may not even be conscious of what they know and what they do. And to understand this, we need to examine what is meant by learning, and how adults learn.

Informal learning and tacit funds of knowledge

Learning is associated in most people's minds with education – with formal school or college. So some people talk about adults 'who have done no learning since leaving school'. Which would mean that, in their minds, those who never went to school have done no learning at all – which of course is nonsense.

For we all know that everybody has done a great deal of learning throughout their lives. All adults – including those who have never been to school - have been learning all the time, in the home and family, in the community, the market, the street and the workplace, in the church or mosque etc – in short, "outside formal educational establishments" (Straka 2004: 3). Indeed, it is clear that "the majority of human learning does not occur in formal contexts" (Eraut 2000: 12); it occurs in daily life.

Much of this learning is **conscious** learning. We set out to learn something, and we pursue strategies which will help us to learn; we search out someone who can help and advise us. Some of us read books or magazines and even look things up on the internet; we may even take lessons (learning a musical instrument, or to drive, for example). But while a good deal of learning is intentional, planned and directed, a great deal of it is unconscious learning. Most of our learning from childhood until the end of life is unplanned, unintended and often unconscious, learning through some activity or play/imagination or social engagement. We set out to solve a problem or complete some task; and we are not conscious at the time of what we have learned, only that we have solved that problem or finished that task more or less satisfactorily.

We can illustrate these two forms of learning by looking at language learning. We all learned our first language unconsciously through engaging with others and imitating them, through play, experiment, trial and error, through struggling to make ourselves understood. Many of us learned a further language more formally – through a teacher who taught us vocabulary and rules of grammar, who controlled and tested our learning. We can call the first kind of learning 'task-conscious' learning – that is, we learn through doing some task; we are conscious of the task but not of the learning, and we measure our success by whether we can complete the task or not. The second kind of learning we can call 'learning-conscious' learning – we know we are learning and we test the result, measure the success in terms of how much we have learned. While not two completely different forms of learning (they form the opposite ends of a continuum), formal and informal learning are different forms of human learning.

Informal learning is being studied more and more. So that we know that through such informal learning, funds of cultural knowledge (Moll et al, 1992) are built up, tacit, unconscious, implicit knowledge. And with this come understandings, skills and especially attitudes which are developed and elaborated over many years, all equally unacknowledged (Polyani 1966; see Reber 1993).

And this is true of both literacy and numeracy: adults have learned much about literacy and numeracy throughout their lives, unconsciously building up funds of knowledge. But, if we were to ask our learners about their existing funds of knowledge and practices, they may not be able to answer since much of what we all know and do on a daily basis is unrecognised, unconscious.

But when they can answer for themselves, we will find that some of their funds of knowledge, their ways of knowing are very different from our own. Nirantar, a women's educational agency in India which pioneered this LETTER approach to adult education, was spurred into taking action when they found that the women with whom they were working held quite different views about the world they lived in from those held by the Nirantar staff who were teaching them. For example, when talking about modern approaches to science with its division of all objects into 'animate' and 'inanimate', the women in their villages said that they regarded rivers as animate, not inanimate. This made Nirantar wish to find out more.

And they felt that asking the women was not enough. What was needed was some way to discover the hidden funds of knowledge and the hidden practices of their women learners and the communities from which they came. So they turned to using ethnographic approaches. The inadequacy of traditional research methods is the main reason why, in this programme of workshops and field work, we adopt an ethnographic approach to trying to learn about the existing literacy and numeracy experiences of our adult learners.

What do we mean by an ethnographic approach?

The workshop participants decided that it is unwise and unnecessary to try to offer firm and universalised definitions of the terms used here such as 'ethnography'. Rather we took the view that a definition need not be a dictionary definition of words but an operational definition that makes the meaning of the ideas clear and useful. An operational definition is a localised, working definition, and avoids the controversial and often unresolvable discussions of a textbook We agreed that what we need is a clarification of key concepts of both ethnography and an ethnographic approach, and of literacy and numeracy.

The working definition of ethnography which our workshops arrived at sees it as a

research approach in which the researcher attempts to understand and represent the beliefs, values and culture of a group or a community in their own terms. Ethnography can be seen as learning about someone else or about something, not from the outside but as far as possible from the inside (Tacchi et al 2003; Hall 2006; Clifford and Marcus 1986). It consists of changing position, adopting a different point of view, trying to see the world through someone else's eyes. As George Openjuru said during the second workshop, *Ethnography is concerned with learning about and understanding different aspect of other people's daily lives, their values, meanings, norms and patterns, and doing this in a way that values them as equal partners in the research process.* Conducting research through an ethnographic perspective means employing participatory ways of sharing knowledge, experience and practices of a community or an individual; and it builds links and bridges between the practices, norms, culture and values of the community with those of the outside world.

Ethnography is unlike other forms of research in that it refers to those forms of social research which have a strong emphasis on *"exploring* the nature of particular social phenomenon rather than *setting out to test* hypotheses about them" (Hammersley and Atkinson, 1995, p. 248). It consists of "close in-depth examinations of social activities as they occur in real life settings" (Papen, 2005, p.59).

> "Ethnography is continuous with ordinary life. Much of what we seek to find out in ethnography is knowledge that others already have. Our ability to learn ethnographically is an extension of what every human being must do, that is, learn the meanings, norms, patterns of a way of life" (Hymes, 1996, p. 13)

Brian Street defined ethnography as the exploration of knowledge that people already have. Ethnography is continuous with everyday life. It refers to learning about the patterns of everyday life. It sounds like very specialist knowledge, but yet we are all ethnographers. All of us have knowledge of our worlds. The question is, 'Who owns the information?'

Brian Street during the first workshop illustrated this need to abandon one's own position and adopt that of another with the story of the turtle and the fish:

"To illustrate the error of ethnocentrism, Buddhists use several versions of the story of the turtle and fish. One story goes like this:

> One day the turtle decides to go for a walk on dry land. He is away from the lake for a few weeks. When he returns, he meets some

fish who ask him: "Mister Turtle, hello! We have not seen you for a few weeks. Where have you been?" The turtle says, "I was up on the dry land." The fish are puzzled: "Up on dry land? What is this dry land? Is it wet?" The turtle answers, "No, it is not." "Is it cool and refreshing?" the fish asks. "No, it is not." "Does it have waves and ripples?" "No, it does not have waves and ripples." "Can you swim in it?" "No, you cannot." So the fish say: "It is not wet, it is not cool, there are no waves, you can't swim in it. So this dry land of yours must be completely non-existent, just an imaginary thing, nothing real at all." The turtle says: "Well, that may be so," and he leaves the fish and goes for another walk on dry land. (www.beyondthenet/dhamma/nibbanaTurtle.htm. accessed April 2007).

We as ethnographers might think of this story in a briefer form. When the turtle returns from dry land to water, and the fish question him, the turtle answers only by saying that the land has no waves, no seaweed, etc. The fish admonish: "Don't tell us what it's **not**, tell us what it **is**!" The longer version of the story is more hopeful than our brief account, for the return "walk on dry land" takes with it refined questions and the intention this time to see what is there" (See Heath and Street 2008).

In ethnography then, we will try to see the dry land still through the eyes of a turtle but one who has come to see that water is not the only context for living, and who is trying to find new words to describe it to himself and to others.

In this search for a way to learn about and describe another world, one of which we have very little experience to guide us, we can suggest that ethnography has a number of characteristics.

1. Ethnography is usually small scale
   It can be seen as looking at one set of activities, at one individual or group in a very concrete way, what has been called 'a thick description' (Geertz 1973). It therefore proceeds by cases – taking one small topic, activity or individual/family or group, and seeking to understand as much as possible about it (Hall 2006: 1). "The basic idea is that one case (or perhaps a small number of cases) will be studied in detail, using whatever methods seem appropriate. While there may be a variety of specific purposes and research questions, the general objective is to develop as full an

understanding of that case as possible" (Punch 1998: 150). Looking at the case studies undertaken by the participants in the LETTER workshops will illustrate this.

2. This case study approach involves looking at the chosen set of activities in detail so that new insights and ways of looking are revealed. Mitchell (1984) sees a case study as "the detailed presentation of ethnographic data relating to some sequence of events from which the analyst seeks to make some theoretical inference". The aim is to stimulate creative thinking.

Each case study is chosen not because it is thought to be typical or a good (or particularly bad) example of some activity but because it is what is called a 'telling case study' (Mitchell 1984). In ethnography, we do not set out to utilise a (random or selective) sample of the population – we take a case study which appeals to us or which is accessible: we choose any case study which tells us something significant about ourselves and the world we live in. We do not claim that our findings apply to anything other than that case study – but we do claim that the findings have some value to the whole field.

Some people have challenged ethnographic approaches on the grounds that these result in what they call 'anecdotal' accounts. As one ethnographer has put, there is a danger we shall forever be imprisoned in particularities. Each case study tells a good story but it does not signify on the wider stage; it lacks validity and reliability; it reveals only partial truth. But ethnography is about different perspectives, views or practices rather than absolute and complete truthfulness, objectivity and complete understanding (Clifford 1986). We can and should use triangulation to check the different information that we are collecting (Miles and Huberman 1994; Yin 1989). However, we are not after universal truth, but examining situations that raise new questions rather than generalisations, collecting alternatives and trying to understand what the implications of these alternatives are for us. As Dave Baker said during the workshop, "We do not have to prove everything; but we do need to raise questions all the time".

3. Can ethnographers claim to generalise? A good case study will enable the researcher to establish theoretically valid connections. Ethnography helps one make a theoretical argument that links

the parts, albeit seemingly unrelated parts, in a coherent way. As we place generalisations and theories together, gradually we "layer up", that is to say, our frame becomes more complicated. So while it is true that as ethnographers we do not try to generalise empirically from one case to many, as in statistical surveys, we do nevertheless try to work out general principles that arise in one case and that offer us insights into other cases.

4. And in doing this, ethnography challenges every generalisation; it tests every assumption used in our own lives. Part of our aim in using ethnographic approaches in LETTER is to test the 'great statements' we all make about literacy and numeracy, to see how far they are true, to "put established conceptions ... into useful question" (Geertz 1988: 21). In what circumstances may this statement **not** be true? To give one example, adult literacy providers tend to make the assumption that all illiterate women are poor, down-trodden, oppressed, cheated and abused. But we found non-educated women who are extremely empowered and we can do little or nothing to empower them any further. As one woman in another context said in regard to her illiteracy and cheating: "Who is going to cheat me? If anyone is going to cheat, it will be me" (Uddin 2006). Or to take as another example the generalisation that "literacy empowers women", an ethnographic case study found that some women working on a farm were not empowered in spite of being literate and more educated than the men on the farm (Prinsloo and Breier 1996); the value system of the farm could not recognise women's education. Literacy does not empower if the context is against such empowerment.

5. Ethnography even challenges itself all the time. Ethnographers adopt a reflexive stance, looking closely at what they are doing and why. What am I doing? Is this the right way to be doing it? What am I bringing to this research? Reflexivity "requires researchers to monitor closely and continually their own interactions with participants" (Cohen et al 2000:141).

The reason for the use of ethnography is that each one of us sees the world through our own lens – a lens which has been built up over many years. And this lens prevents us from seeing many things that are there. The ethnographer will ask, 'What lens am I using for seeing people's practices and cultural behaviour?' As ethnographers, we start with our own lens. We come to see that we make assumptions without having any real evidence. Where is the evidence for the generalisations I am making? How can I get this evidence? In adopting an ethnographic approach, we try to identify and then (as far as we can) abandon our own assumptions and adopt another person's view. That is why some anthropologists insist on ethnography taking a long time, to give the researcher time to become conscious of and move away from his/her own assumptions.

6. Ethnography then is turning my world upside down to try to take the point of view of another person. Ethnography is about understanding an activity through someone else's eyes. It can be seen as changing position, trying to see the world as someone else sees it; it is learning about someone else or about something, not from the outside but as far as possible from the inside.

One danger of the story of the turtle and the fish is that it may suggest that an ethnographer is only interested in the strange, the 'other' – in 'making the strange familiar'. But ethnography will also look at what is to us 'normal'. The turtle could use ethnography to look at the fish as well as the strange dry land; it can be used **to** 'make the familiar strange', to "shift attention from the exotic 'other' to [our] own society" (Clifford 1986: 9). It has been suggested that ethnography can be seen as engaging with the experience near through the experience distant (Geertz 1988).

Putting people into two categories of 'literate' and 'illiterate' means that there is a danger that only illiterates tend to be studied. But as George Openjuru said in relation to our study of local literacy and numeracy practices,

> " Ethnography is not only about indigenous knowledge systems, but also about what all people are doing. We are not questioning aspects of how primitive people are negotiating modern systems of knowledge. We live in a literate environment and we all have to interact with the written world. There are certain aspects of our lives that interact with the written world and we need to investigate these things, what practices are we using to deal with this?" Ethnography is not just about those who are not literate; it will need to cover the whole spectrum of literacy in the community.

We do want to stress this, because all existing adult literacy learning programmes are aimed at those who are defined as being 'illiterate'. This is of course natural, for there is in all adult literacy learning programmes a tendency to focus on non-literates and to ignore those who are literate, finding out what and how they are reading and writing. Yet what the literate people are doing is a large part of what constitutes the literacy practices of that community and it is that which will be relevant to any literacy learner coming from that community. Certainly we saw the need to discover how the so-called 'literate' were using their literacy skills. Our ethnographic concern is not only with the coping methods that are being employed by the non-literates in the community but with how literacy is being used throughout the whole community. For this will form a large part of the experience of the literacy learners.

7. Within this field, however, we cannot decide in advance exactly what we are looking for (although we have the general field of study), because we do not know what is important to the other. An ethnographer avoids determining in advance what to look for, imposing his/her value system on the informants; rather they seek to understand "how people experience and feel events in their lives", how they make sense of their world and themselves (Beins 2004). For example, one of our case studies explored attitudes towards the benefits of microfinance through the eyes of women borrowers, and found one person who said she "hated it." In one or two of the case studies, the respondents were said to be 'illiterate'; but in most cases, this is the researcher speaking. Instead of making such judgments, looking down on other people and saying, 'We can help you', we are trying to understand them, to see their value and belief systems. By getting as close to the respondent(s) as possible, we are trying to make the things that are important to them become important to us. We must not underestimate how difficult this is – it takes time and we will never do it completely, but this is what we attempt to do.

8. But even while doing this, the researcher remains conscious of her/himself. Through reflexivity, we are aware of the reason for undertaking the research in the first place, of the experience, beliefs and values which we bring to the task - in our case, of identifying and understanding the literacy and numeracy practices which the learners do within their own community, practices of which the

researched may be completely unconscious. The researcher goes back and forth – enters the situation and then retreats to consider before re-entering again. "Ethnography should be considered as cyclical, with forward and backward movement," as Brian Street said during the workshop. It is not a question of the researcher abandoning his/her own belief systems and values but as Todorov and others have suggested (Todorov 1988; Geertz 1988), a "paradoxical sense of distance and closeness", a continuous process of movement backwards and forwards that one probably never gets out of, once acquired. The terms, *'emic'* and *'etic'*, taken from the field of linguistic studies, are often used in the field of anthropology to describe this proximity/distance relationship. Thus *'emic'* is used to describe the insider's point of view, while *'etic'* is used for the outsider's point of view. The ethnographer does not simply try to capture the local but rather tries to understand their way of understanding, using an *emic/etic* approach, not as either/or but exploring how the local and the outsider views are related. The *emic* sheds light on the local perspective, and the *etic* account may see it from outside, but the *emic/etic* axis or relationship will relate the two together.

9. Ethnography does not even take the statements expressed by the informants as conclusive but tries to find out what they mean by what they are saying. Argyris and Schon (1975) have pointed to the gap between what they call 'the espoused theory' (the reason we all give for our actions) and the 'theory-in-practice' (the real reason we act as we do). An ethnographic approach involves unpacking everything, questioning 'why?' and again 'why?' until there is no further 'why?'. In particular, it includes 'observation', watching and following sometimes over extended periods to see what happens which the researched may not even notice. Sometimes this will mean 'participant observation', joining in some activity to *feel* what it is like.

10. Ethnography looks for both differences and conformity. And when it finds difference, it does not count this as deficit. The title of a recent book, *Celebrating the Other*, reminds us that 'the other' is not inferior but different. An ethnographic approach does not judge the other but values the other as equal but different. We need to leave our own normative position, that is, the feeling that what we are is the best and should be the norm or the rule by which all

other people must be qualified or disqualified. Rather, we seek to value their difference, not assess their 'lack' of something or their not knowing.

11. And we construct our own picture from what we see, what we touch and what we hear. We imply meaning to what we find – and try to describe it to others. We are not trying to find objective 'truth' but to draw a picture through our own lens (Hall 2006: 3-4). It is our picture – other people will see other things which we may miss or which will not seem so important to us.

To do that, we use language – our language. When we use certain words, we often assume that the meaning is shared. However, sometimes meaning is interpreted differently by different audiences. Sometimes we will observe something and describe it, assuming that the listener/reader understands. But we all know from experience that this is not necessarily true. Ethnography sometimes requires us to describe what may seem to be obvious but in language which is unusual.

An ethnography or an ethnographic approach?

There is a distinction between three approaches to carrying out ethnographic work.

Conducting Ethnography: refers to framing and conceptualising through an in-depth long-term study of a social group. It is particularly anthropologists have "owned" this approach.

Adopting an Ethnographic Perspective: refers to applying an ethnographic approach to a specific situation. This approach is less comprehensive than a full ethnography and more appropriately describes what the participants were attempting to engage in through the LETTER Workshop process. It is a general impulse to notice, to listen, to ask questions, and to reflect which probably once gained is never lost.

Adopting Ethnographic Tools: refers to using the tools of observation and participant observation to comprehend a certain situation but without the general theory of culture and society that is involved in either of the other two approaches.

The first is characterised by the pure anthropologist who travels to an area and stays there for a number of years and then writes a major study on a community. However, there is a middle ground between highly specialised skills and the ethnography that we all learn as members of society. This can be characterised by disciplined and reflective ethnographic inquiry in which an ethnographic perspective is systematically applied to specific situations and processes (Green and Bloome 1997)

Changing the situation?

Ethnography also involves different levels of involvement or 'interference'. An ethnographic approach is different from traditional research which says, "I need to stand back from this activity and look at it." For the ethnographer is aware that, in both observation and participant observation, the researcher's presence impacts what is going on: he/she is not just a 'fly on the wall'. Those being 'observed' may adapt their behaviour because of the researcher's presence. There are different views regarding the appropriateness of "interference" in ethnography, but an ethnographer's approach to research means that she/he knows that there is always the chance that her/his presence may interfere with the activity that is being observed. The recently developed field of Public Interest Anthropology assumes that the ethnographer has an obligation to get involved and try to change things. To say one is not interfering is to miss the point that doing ethnography is an engagement with other people and their way of life.

Who should engage in ethnography and when?

The workshop looked at these two questions and came to the following conclusions.

Who? In our context, we see an ethnographic approach as being necessary for the facilitators or instructors in order for them to learn about the existing literacy and numeracy practices of their learners and the community from which they come. But we also see the literacy learners using such approaches to learn about their own literacy and numeracy practices – becoming critically reflective as they become conscious of their own unconscious funds of knowledge and the literacy and numeracy practices they engage in.

And when? An ethnographic stance, once acquired, remains with one for life. It becomes natural to enquire into the practices of other people, to try to understand not only their practices but our own.

Some such research will be deliberately pursued to solve a problem; but other research will take place during the course of any activity. Ethnography is (as we will see below) a frame of mind, not a special activity.

Why use an ethnographic approach

We have seen above that traditional approaches to research do not yield results in terms of revealing the hidden funds of knowledge which the learners bring to their literacy and numeracy learning. Using ethnographic approaches is more likely to provide the information we need to build new and more effective learning programmes for adults.

But we are not saying that ethnography should replace all other forms of research. We see it (like other forms of qualitative research) as an additional tool for researchers, and for planners and teachers, a way of adding depth to other studies, a means of testing the findings of more quantitative research.

And it can also be seen as a way of looking at all research – a participatory process which tries to make meaning out of the findings of other (more quantitative) researchers in terms of the researched.

Ethnography as a window on literacy and numeracy

This becomes particularly clear when we look at the role of ethnography in developing a deeper understanding of literacy and numeracy.

Taking an ethnographic approach to literacy and numeracy means that we start from the premise that people already have literacy practices. The question for adult educators is, 'How do we build on these practices?' This question is different from assuming that people have no pre-existing literacy. But when we look at literacy in real life, we see that the word 'literacy' is used in many different ways. For example, some staff in some universities say, "The students these days are illiterate." This usage is different from the use of the word 'illiterate' in other contexts, particularly in a developing country context.

An ethnographic approach to literacy then does not start by assuming that people are not literate. Rather, it seeks to discover *what literacy activities there are in any society and how different people relate to these activities*. Our first question will then be, "Are they using literacy in some ways?" There are many different modes of communication, but people may not use all of them; which mode a person uses is a choice, whether conscious or unconscious.

Our researches have shown us that there are local literacy and numeracy practices, what a recent book has termed 'hidden literacies', that have been overlooked. When adult and non-formal educators try to persuade people to become 'literate', the question arises, "which literacy?" We need to recognise the different kinds of literacies people have.

For instance, along the drive from the Addis Ababa to the training centre in Yirgalem, a variety of languages were seen being utilised. Brian Street questioned the use of scripts when he noticed that Isuzu cargo trucks had the word Isuzu inscribed in both Arabic and Latin scripts on the back of many trucks. Multilingualism and multi-scriptism are then built into the experience of being literate in Ethiopia in a way that it is not in other places. If we walk around the town of Bahir Dar, what can we learn about literacy practices? Are local people taking for granted that signs will be written in a number of different languages and scripts whilst to outsiders this needs explaining and is not necessarily 'normal'? Which script is used for which kind of sign? Local people are making complex choices all the time but visitors – like the turtle upon dry land – need help with understanding what they mean.

Identifying different literacy practices

Such choices when studied begin to fall into patterns, what are called 'literacy (and numeracy) practices'. In engaging in any study of literacy, it is useful to draw a distinction between a literacy event and a literacy practice.

A literacy event is a specific event, a one-off occurrence of literacy involving some text.

A literacy practice is a repeated behaviour, a demonstrable pattern that continues to occur – it shapes the literacy events, just as the literacy events accumulate to make up the literacy practices. .

A similar distinction may be developed with respect to numeracy, namely between numeracy events and numeracy practices.

In ethnography, it is important to go beyond the individual literacy and numeracy events to connect them into a practice, to move from the particular into the broader field. And doing this, it is possible to identify different kinds of literacy practices.

Brian Street (1984) found in his area of Iran three main kinds of literacy practices - *commercial literacy practices* found among the shop keepers, *religious literacy practices* widely throughout the community, and the more limited *schooled literacy practices* used by the educated. The commercial and religious literacy practices in his case were linked together but the schooled literacy practices were more separate. These insights provided questions that can be asked in other contexts, including Ethiopia as members of the workshops walked around Yergalem and Bahir Dar and observed literacy in mosques, churches, schools, shops, streets, markets etc.

These are the public literacy practices. But there are others less public – domestic and family literacy practices. Collecting stories about people's lives can help to find and identify these more private literacy practices. In a book called *African Hidden Histories*, historians and ethnographers document the phenomenon of 'tin trunk literacy', where community members were found to have kept a host of letters, diaries, agendas and other literacy materials in tin trunks. Many houses have texts of some kind on their walls, even when they cannot be read. This phenomenon has encouraged literacy ethnographers to ask, 'Is there a local history of literacy that is hidden? Are people doing things that we have not even thought about?' This can be seen elsewhere. In one area in Japan, literacy seemed to have blossomed, and researchers wanted to know why. They found that much earlier, books had been distributed to each household. No instructions were given. The people wondered if they were going to be punished if they did not read the books; they inquired but were not able to find out. Because they couldn't find the answer, they just started reading, using their own devices.

Ethnographic studies of literacy and language have uncovered the importance of the role of the 'mediator'. In Mexico, for example, researchers saw how people go to scribes in the plaza who mediate and write down information and legal documents for them (Kalman 1999). In Ethiopia, such mediation can be seen in a bank or post office when an officer on duty fills a form out for a client. Literate clients have sometimes found this process frustrating because it is time-consuming to repeat each address and telephone number and the client could have filled out the form in a fraction of the time. However, since many people do not have literacy skills or bureaucracy navigation skills, a system has developed which assumes all clients come without these skills and thus need mediation. Without having to question the client and embarrass them to disclose whether they are 'literate' or 'illiterate', the officer behind the desk instead mediates for all. Ethnography helps to identify these local literacy practices.

And ethnography reveals that these local literacy practices are tied up within the existing power systems of the society. In one case in Ethiopia, programme implementers found in one community that people who had control over writing had control of the land. Therefore some farmers were not able to get access to this land. The literacy programme implementers engaged with these farmers, so that they gained the appropriate literacy skills for claiming land.

The models of what counts as literacy are changing. The narrow definition of literacy used in the UNESCO and other international literacy learning programmes of previous decades as meaning only schooled literacy led to these programmes failing to achieve their objectives. This understanding was overtaken by Freirean literacy which again saw 'literacy' as something which had to be introduced into the local community rather than a set of practices which were already in the local community. For in both cases, as our case studies show, many of these local practices are not regarded, either by the providers or by those in the community who use them, as 'proper literacy'. They are 'informal' (vernacular, indigenous) literacy practices, not 'your sort of literacy' as one informant put it. Ethnography can show in greater detail how different cultural models of language and literacy manifest themselves in each different set of circumstances.

Developing community literacy learning programmes: And as we have seen, such findings can form the basis of developing a more effective adult learning programme to enhance the use of literacy throughout the community. This is of course a rather different approach from the traditional adult literacy learning programme. The two elements in an ethnography of literacy – identifying the different literacy practices, both formal and informal, being used in the community as a whole, and identifying how the non-literate are negotiating these literacy practices - will in turn lead to two closely related literacy learning programmes, both of which will aim to help the participants to learn to use literacy and written forms of numeracy more effectively in their daily lives. The 'literate' as well as the non-literate need to learn more useful ways of using texts to record and plan, monitor and evaluate their activities. That is part of a much wider brief for adult literacy than simply introducing reading and writing into a particular context; it is introducing the culture of *effectively using* reading and writing to improve performance in life's projects. As our case studies showed us, many people, literate and non-literate alike, are still being informed by *non-literate* practices in real life; for example, many are not using their literacy in their livelihood activities. Schools and adult education learning programmes are not attending to this, since they focus on learning to pass exams and not on the ways literacy is used in daily life. So the primary focus and concern of an ethnographic approach to literacy and numeracy learning is to find out and understand local ways that can improve the use of literacy in life's projects for the purpose of improving people's performance in those projects.

The value then of ethnographic approaches to literacy and numeracy is that only through this kind of approach can local literacy and numeracy practices be identified and used as the basis for building new adult learning programmes and developing new forms of teaching-learning materials. Discussion of these issues led the workshop participants to explore the need to conduct lobbying work with those creating all kinds of literacy materials, so that material developers can receive cultural advice based on ethnographic research about the appropriateness of what is being produced.

How do we use ethnographic approaches – tools and methods

In discussing how to conduct ethnographic-style research into literacy and numeracy practices, the LETTER workshops distinguished between three issues – ethnographic technique, ethnographic tools and ethnographic methods.

Ethnographic Technique

A recent book by Shirley Brice Heath and Brian Street *On Ethnography* (2008) has compared ethnography to juggling. "It isn't a technique that you suddenly do. It is a technique that is slowly learned and absorbed". So too an ethnographic technique can be developed slowly over time; it is more a frame of mind than a set of methods to be applied mechanically.

Among the attitudes which the workshop participants identified as characterising ethnographic style research are the following: valuing the community and its practices, a non-patronising approach, respect and politeness, a willingness to listen attentively, and above all the attitude of being an inquirer, a learner, of not being satisfied with one's own presuppositions, a questioning of one's own assumptions. There are in all ethnographic research major ethical considerations.

And yet at the same time, the belief and value systems of the researcher are not suppressed in a search for objective truth and an unbiased account. Through reflexivity, ethnographic researchers are conscious of their own assumptions, their own values, their ideas and positions on numeracy and literacy and those of the informants. To detect one's own assumptions, one must be conscious of them: we need to know ourself. What assumptions am I making about other people and about myself?

In addition, ethnographic researchers will be conscious of the wider aspects of their research. For example, there is the language in which it is conducted – not just the tongue but also the register. They will be conscious of the cultural gap between themselves and the researched – a gap caused by factors such as education, residence, dress and mobility (arriving in a vehicle will create all kinds of expectations on the part of the researched). But such features do not make the researcher superior to the researched. As Dave Baker reminded the workshop participants,

> "We who are educated are more restricted and in deficit compared with the rural people who are able to translate from the rural and traditional [measures] to the standard. Part of ethnography is observing the gap between you the researcher and the one who is the centre of the ethnography."

Throughout the whole research will be issues of power. The researchers will tend to control the process, dictate the topics to be discussed, select the items they want, and can leave the research context at any time they wish to do so. Mutual respect will need to be created to complete the task successfully.

Ethnographic research then is the coming together of two unequal partners, researched and researcher, to consider the topic area under consideration. In doing ethnographic research, the co-operation of the community will need to be secured. Ethnographic research is more than just 'hanging about' (as some have designated it) although that is a large part of it. It means staying with the people and participating in the activities of life in which the researcher is interested so as to understand them; to observe them very carefully and ask questions that can help one to understand them.

Ethnographic methodology

A great deal was said during the workshops about the methods of ethnography. Some of the participants saw ethnography in terms of a tool box to be picked up and used in their own situation rather than a substantial change of attitude. But as their attitudes changed, there came certain methodologies which proved useful.

Although they are different, 'method' and 'tool' in ethnography are often used synonymously. In our approach, 'method' is considered as a broader concept to mean ways of doing things, while 'tool' is considered as an instrument to put into practice the method. Whatever method we have adopted, there are some instruments with which we are able to implement that method. Within this context, what follows aims at providing an introduction to some applicable methods and tools to carry out an ethnographic study.

Ethnographic studies of literacy and numeracy practices will imply a multi-method approach involving the use of extensive (wide) and intensive (deep) key informant interviews (sometimes known as biographical methods), participant observation, and collecting and analysing documentary evidence of literacy in the community. Other methods involve the use of film, videos and photographs to provide visual data and the collection of artefacts where relevant. There is no one set of tools and methods – different contexts and themes will call for different methods to be used.

There are alternative ways of doing ethnographic study. One can choose a method or multiple methods based on mainly four issues, namely: the researcher, the researched, the theme of the research, and the environment. The method(s) chosen should fit the ability and experience of the researcher, the culture and norms of the researched, the subject under scrutiny, and the prevailing context of the study.

As our field work showed, the ways of investigating the literacy and numeracy practices in a church, in the market or with a local institution like an Edir (funeral club) are clearly different.

The following are some of the appropriate methods that can be used for ethnographic study.

- Observation
- Collecting documentary evidence and artefacts
- Photography and videoing
- In-depth interviews (and taping interviews)
- Focus group discussion
- PRA-Transect walk / social mapping

1. Observation refers to the technique of watching what is going on. Observation is the most important method which gives us a chance to look into the existing condition of the environment and people. This adds an important dimension to the more normal process of interviewing (Atkinson et al 2003: 112-114). Interviewing seeks to find out the inner dimensions of the respondents' lives; observation seeks to identify the social interactions in which that inner life is expressed. It is through watching and provoking into action, balanced against what is said, that a fuller picture can be built up.

Among the things we identified to look for in a literacy and numeracy survey are:

- *Settings*: The physical and temporal circumstances as well as settlements of the community
- *People* who interact (or do not interact) with the written texts; those who are involved in the social relationships of producing, interpreting, circulating and otherwise regulating written texts
- *Activities*: Actions, routines, strategies, rules as to what is appropriate and eligibility; who are included and who excluded
- *Resources*: Material artefacts, tools, accessories, all other resources brought to the literacy and numeracy practices including non-material values, understandings, ways of

thinking, feeling, technical skills and knowledge; beliefs, representational (semiotic) resources
- *The different scripts and symbols* with which the community is interacting
- *Ways of communications* that are practised by the community in their daily life
- *Domains or institutions*: Existing formal and informal institutions as well as fields of social or institutional practice within which events take place and from which they take their sense and social purpose.

Some important tools used during observation include photography, pictures, drawings, village walk, maps, etc.

Participation Observation refers to the ethnographer joining in the activities of the group being observed. This will help to create a climate in which new relationships can be built and result in a greater participation of the researched in the research. An example was given by one of the participants in local terms: Some extension workers had found that sometimes gypsies with whom they were working had decided not to answer questions or not to answer correctly because they feared that the questioner might be trying to persuade them to settle down, to stop travelling or may trick them in some way. An anthropologist who wanted to explore the life of gypsies, instead of directly questioning them, took up the business of selling second-hand goods. She found that the gypsies began to associate with her and explain what she was doing wrong. One way of learning as an ethnographer is to start doing something wrong and allow others to correct you; the people being researched are the ones with the knowledge and expertise and the researcher is the learner.

2. Interviewing: Much ethnography is based on information provided by the researched, either individually in an interview (semi-structured or unstructured) or in a focus group discussion (Kvale 1996). There are of course limits to this; it is sometimes better not to ask direct questions. People may be suspicious of outsiders' motives and they may, in any case, use different terms to describe their experience.

But having a conversation with a person from whom we want to learn or collect data is inevitable when conducting an ethnographic study.

However, as the purpose of ethnographic study is to learn how things are, what are matters of priority to them, how people are managing their life, the traditional method of interview seems inappropriate. In a formal interview, be it semi-structured or structured, the researcher has some agenda to deal with or investigate. But the interview in an ethnographic study, in which the study theme may come out of the blue and not necessarily only in the form of a planned study, is very different. Ethnographic researchers neither ask a set of pre-designed questions, nor simply follow a pre-designed checklist. They rather explore, asking a chain of questions or chasing a theme to learn about people's life in depth. The key activities here are not so much the *asking* as the *listening* and *recording* of what is said and done, especially the words being used as far as possible, the language in which the statements are being made.

But the ethnographic researcher will in one sense be more proactive than the traditional researcher. The traditional researchers ask pre-determined questions for the purpose of collecting information, and they accept what the respondent says and record it. But ethnographic researchers do not always accept what is said at face value: they will seek to obtain *examples* of what the respondent is saying, concrete instances in their lives when the stated behaviour actually operates. To give one or two examples: if, when talking about the benefits of learning literacy, the informant says, "We can now read the places on the bus", the ethnographic researcher will press for an actual example of that behaviour; if the informant says that she can now write a letter, the ethnographic researcher will press for the last time such a letter was written, to whom and what was the subject of it, etc. Examples of such written texts may even be collected. The researcher in ethnography seeks the detailed life stories which reveal the reality, not what the respondents believe is happening.

Some important tools used during interviews: notebook, pen, pencil, audio recording (if possible with the permission of the respondents)

3. Small group discussion: in ethnographic study, not only individuals but groups of people are also considered as sources of information. This is not just a group interview but the group members on their own will engage in discussion, every now and again prompted by the researcher. Researchers will seek to spark discussion in line with the real life of the community and their engagement in any

form of literacy and numeracy activities. The discussion will not be limited to existing literacy and numeracy practices; it will be free to roam over other aspects of the group's lives in the context of that specific society and locality. Although the size of the group depends on various factors, the researcher should note that the smaller the group, the more interactive and participatory will be the discussion – but it can on occasion also be too small.

Focus groups have considerable value not only for the researchers but for the researched. "Focus groups tend to create environments in which participants feel open to telling their stories and to giving their testimonies in front of other women like themselves" (Madriz, 2003: 383). But it is important to appreciate that a focus group is not simply a group interview. In a focus group, the emphasis is on the interactions between the group members and not just with the researcher. A focus group is concerned with "the joint construction of meaning" (Bryman 2004: 346) – that is, through the discussion initiated by the researcher, the group members come to some new insights for themselves.

"Interviews may be more appropriate for tapping into individual biographies, but focus groups are more suitable for examining how knowledge, and more importantly, ideas, develop and operate within a given cultural context. Questionnaires are more appropriate for obtaining quantitative information and explaining how many people hold a certain (pre-defined) opinion: focus groups are better for exploring exactly how those opinions are constructed" (Wilkinson and Kitzinger, 1995: 9)

Some important tools used during small group discussion: notebook, pen, pencil, audio recording, video etc (if possible with the permission of the respondents)

4. Visual representation: It would be very useful to supplement the collected data (quantitative and qualitative) from the study area with visual representations. Visual information is important to refresh our memories after returning back from field. In addition to this, they are crucial tools to triangulate the data we have collected using other methods. Collecting items from the research location such as texts, copies of writing, labels etc are an important part of ethnographic research methods. Such visual material is likely to provide an important piece of information which was not seen during the field work on site. PRA has sometimes been used

to prepare visual representations of the information which the respondents reveal, indeed for helping them to become aware for the first time of certain aspects of their own daily lives (Guijt and Cornwall 1995; Cornwall et al 2001).

Some important tools used for visual representation: still camera, video camera, picture and drawings, scripts, etc.

5. Documentary survey: Collecting and analysing all the documents that can be found in relation to the chosen case study is of course an imperative (Burns 2000; Yin 1994). This will range from the very formal (government papers and other official reports) to the very informal (texts written on all kinds of surfaces). But the importance of these documents is not that they are authoritative; they provide a perspective which information collected from other sources can corroborate or challenge.

Apart from the methods presented above, researchers are free to adopt other innovative and participatory methods of data collection for ethnographic research for example, material from the general environment concerning ways of communication.

Field Work

The major component of ethnographic research is fieldwork – going to a community to see what happens rather than reading about it from a distance.

Snatch case studies: We do need to recognise that some ethnographic research does not come from a deliberately planned research programme; it may just arise. As Dr Rafat Nabi said in the workshop about her case studies in Pakistan, "Before going to the field, I chose only one case study, that is the glass bangle seller. The rest of the examples were not chosen by me before going into the field. These cases came so strongly and naturally into my way that I could not avoid them. I saw something worthwhile when I was talking to them and decided to write about them". Two of the case studies in this book are of this nature – what might be called 'snatch case studies', in which an unexpected incident occurs and the ethnographer snatches at it since it offers a special insight into some aspect of the general field of enquiry.

Planned field work: But most fieldwork for ethnographic research will be planned in advance. The following are some notes developed by the workshop participants to conduct fieldwork.

The first step is to choose both the theme and the site to be examined. In our case, *the area of study or theme* is the value, meanings and uses of literacy and numeracy in the local community, leading to an understanding of the differences and similarities between the researchers and the researched in terms of their activities, roles, needs, funds of knowledge and experiences. We wanted to identify local literacy and numeracy events and practices, and to see how these interrelate with formal school literacy. But whatever the theme, if working with others, we need to make sure that all members of the research team have a thorough understanding of the theme and objective of the research.

With reference to the site, since we are looking for a telling case study rather than typicality or representativeness, the major criteria might well be accessibility. The case studies in this book arose in many cases through contacts made during the course of the normal work of the workshop participants.

Before going into the field, it will be useful if the researcher, having identified the theme and selected the site, prepares a checklist and collects background information on things like the official adult literacy rate, what is already known (or assumed) about their existing practices and indigenous knowledge, the interest of the community, the various community-based organisations (CBOs), local government and religious institutions etc working in the area. A map will usually be essential. We will need to check on language issues, for we may need a translator or mediator. It will be useful to enquire into local issues which may hinder the research work, such as public holidays or major events which may make the informants unavailable. It will almost always be necessary to acquire some form of permission, either to conduct the research in that location or to use the information obtained from the researched for our own purposes – and permission especially for taking and using photographs and recording voices. We need to bear in mind the ethics of field visits. It may be useful to draw up a brief statement about the research to hand out; but personal explanations are far better; since in many circumstances a written statement will sound too formal to establish trust and shared concerns. In every case, it is important to explain one's objectives to interviewees and properly introduce oneself to the "gatekeepers".

Some preparation in advance of data gathering tools (observation, questionnaire, informal dialogue, interview, etc.) will be useful, but it is important that these do not become restrictive to the research project – it must be open-ended and free-flowing.

We need to note that ethnographic research rarely goes smoothly, especially at the beginning. Many of our case studies started out in one way and had to be changed for many reasons. As George Openjuru told the participants, they may have a bright idea, and go to the community; but new experiences will emerge and then they will come to realise that the original idea might not be right for those circumstances. If they discover situations that shatter their original conceptions, they will need to come back and reformulate their original ideas. Our case studies carefully recorded this when it happened so as to indicate the way in which the case study came about.

The length of time spent in the field will of course vary; and it may be necessary to go back to check or to gather further information.

During the fieldwork, the aim is to learn what is going on. We are seeking to collect evidence of the learners' numeracy and literacy practices through events that the people engage in and through the texts they have produced or used. We therefore need to find ways of identifying these events through observations, conversations and engagement with the practices rather than through formal assessment (testing, questioning, completing forms).

When looking at what is going on, it will be useful to adopt what is called an 'extended framework' rather than a narrow focus. In looking at numeracy and literacy, we need to adopt a broad social practice view of numeracy and literacy. If we were to use a narrow one, we would notice only a few things. We would see the skills used and not see the social relations, pressures, roles etc; we would tend to express our findings in terms of deficit and exclusion based on a particular view of literacy and numeracy rather than a more positive description. An extended framework gives richer data which goes beyond formal skills and texts or numbers to literacy and numeracy practices.

Fieldwork is based on the twin principles of listen and observe. We need to look round the total environment at signs and public texts, at language and signs - and watch the interactions with these texts and signs. Studying people's interaction will provide clues to what is informing their behaviour. We must try to see below the surface, and not be content with those elements which can be seen and heard. We want to discover the norms, values and beliefs of the people we are investigating, to find out their (unconscious) funds of knowledge. This is the extended framework.

Unless absolutely necessary, the researcher should not interfere with the activities that the individuals of the area are performing, but simply observe. The objective is to describe the situation as it is, not to alter it to suit our requirements. Nevertheless, some activities will sometimes help to promote the research. Some of the workshop participants bought items from the market stalls; they compared the informal local measures used in different parts of the markets with the standardised measures. Throughout all our research, however much we try to avoid involvement, we need to be aware that our very presence is going to change things and influence the situation.

And above all, an ethnographer will ask questions – usually in the form of "Why…?".

> As George Openjuru put it, Ask what may appear stupid questions politely if the meaning of some actions are not clear. You should ask questions the way the monkey does. He stops, faces you square and looks at you. Then he moves around and stops and looks again. Then he climbs a tree and looks at you from the top. Then he takes a good long look at your backside.

Questioning in this way depends on the relationship built up between researched and researchers. Ethnographic research is based on the establishment of mutual respect between the parties – the informants become partners in the research. Creating this relationship will usually take time and certainly takes effort. Introducing oneself and explaining the purpose of the visit will defuse some of the suspicion and fear. Participating in what they are doing (depending on the type of activity) will often help. An ethnographer will always seek to take time - there is no rush.

Field Notes

While watching, listening and asking questions, we also need to be recording - taking notes, if acceptable and it is not disruptive, in an unobtrusive way, without attracting attention to what we are doing.

The products of our ethnographic research are our field notes. These are very important (Eisenhardt 1989).

Our notes should be as detailed as we can possibly make them. We must not forget to record the time and the context of the observation, the when and where - indeed to note everything that happens during the process of data collection as far as we can. Detailed field notes should include subject matter even if at the time we think that it is not relevant; we can decide afterwards what is relevant or irrelevant. Experience informs us that we should not believe ourselves when we say, "I will remember that". We won't.

To keep our notes brief, we can use abbreviations and our own form of shorthand. When taking notes, we need to develop a system to distinguish between recording things that actually happened and noting down those things that we think about while looking. We can make what are sometimes called 'headnotes' for ourselves – those personal comments we want to make on what we see and hear. Some people divide their notebook into two columns, one side for recording what is going on, the other for personal thoughts; others put such notes into the text but marked off in some way (square brackets, for example, or underlined) or find some other way to ensure that passing comments are not lost.

Apart from making notes, there are other forms of documentation of what we observe which we will need to use, such as video and photographs and collecting samples wherever possible. But we do need to remember that sometimes people pull back when they see a tape recorder, and be careful about choosing when to use a tape recorder. We must always get permission to record and to take photographs.

Writing up

After the fieldwork there comes two or three further stages.

1. First, there will be the writing up of our field notes – making our rough notes into usable notes. This should be done as soon as possible after the field work. We will be surprised at how many queries we will find as we go through our notes. We must be prepared to go back to the field if need be

2. Then comes the writing up of our case studies, presenting a story of what happened. This is one stage of refinement beyond our

field notes which record what we did and what we saw and heard in sequence. Writing up the case study will involve selecting items from our notes so as to make a consecutive narrative out of the dispersed notes. It is important to include as much background information as possible to help the readers. Case studies will provide detailed accounts (vignettes) of actual processes and should include the voices of the participants – both researcher and researched. Throughout the process, we need to place ourselves in the communities' place and see things from their point of view.

3. Then comes the final and most difficult part, the analysis, drawing conclusions from the findings. Once the data has been collected and arranged, it can be analysed (Miles and Huberman 1994) . This process involves understanding the meaning of the data collected. We seek to understand the literacy and numeracy practices discovered in terms of the values, social relations, contexts involved in these practices.

This analysis normally takes the form of detailed description and explanation of the data. We need to be as descriptive as possible, remembering that we want a 'thick' description. We have to pick out and show what seems to be the key evidence as clearly as possible, and describe the patterns and themes that are evident in the data. We are looking for evidence relating to the themes which fit the objectives of our study.

The analysis and sorting into different categories is one of the most important phases of the research. There are many methods used to analyse ethnographic data. Among these are the following:

- *Thematic analysis* (or coding data into categories) – separating out different themes from all the material collected. For example, different forms of counting or measuring.

- *Textual analysis* of interview transcripts and documents – what did they say and why did they say it, especially why did they say it in that way? Example: "You are illiterate?" – Response: "Yes, I have never been to school", would indicate that the respondent assumes that 'literacy' means 'going to school'.

- *Content analysis* (discourse analysis) – comparing where different informants talk about similar topics but use different words to express their ideas, how the language they use reveals the world picture they have in their minds, often unconsciously.

- *Photographic analysis* – looking for things in the background which could have been missed while you were there.

In all these and in other forms of analysis, the most important thing is for us to see patterns and seek to answer the question 'why'. And through it all, we will need to be reflective about our perception of and our impact on the research outcomes and conclusions.

Some of us found that one way to work on our notes was to use highlighter pens or post-it notes, etc. Others found it helpful to use one colour for one theme. Such devices will help us to draw conclusions and to use the collected data systematically.

In our case studies, thematic analysis seems to be the most useful way to produce the conclusions we have drawn.

Writing up the report

Data analysis will be followed by writing the report.

Ethnography involves collecting data about those being studied. This data can be spoken, written, visual or physical. However, ethnography is not just about collecting data but also about presenting data or materials. This may mean first, speaking about the data to others, second, demonstrating with visual aids, and third, writing for others.

There is no one way to write an ethnographic report, for just as the research is individual, so the report will be individual. But to help the workshop participants, Brian Street suggested that ethnographic presentations should deal with the following areas:

- Framing
- Methodology
- Data
- Themes

Framing: In order to communicate unfamiliar data to an audience, the data needs to be appropriately framed. What do we need to tell the audience so that they are on the same page and have enough context to comprehend? This is often one of the major problems with presentations on ethnography, that the research does not make the imaginative link to the audience, that the presentation does not give enough information to someone who was not there or who does not understand the background. Each report should contain background information – a short and precise introduction setting out both the context and the objective(s) of the study, why it was done; and the methodology used.

Methodology: This section should explain why exactly the researcher chose to use certain information-gathering techniques, e.g. interviews, observation, tape recording, photographs etc. This section should also contain a discussion of what actually happened when the techniques were used and the issues that arose, for instance, ethical issues, photographing issues, and so forth.

Data: There will never be enough time and space to present all the data that we will have collected. The data is potentially open ended. The categories are not necessarily there and we need to cull through the data to identify themes. Like a sieve, we need to pull out the hay, stones and dirt, i.e. the things that are not relevant to the themes we are exploring.

Themes: In moving from data to themes, we are on provisional grounds. Looking at the data, we must see if we can identify a theme and then can justify it. The identification of themes is not an attempt to present the whole of what we have found. In the time and space available, we may be only able to present one or two themes.

Condensing the presentation of an ethnographic study into a limited space-time forces discipline. Consolidation will be necessary in making our presentation precise. Ethnographic material must be cut down. It is as if we have to present our life's story in 15 minutes.

Our case studies are designed to be 'telling' case studies; so the report will include a section on 'what does this case study *tell* me?' But we hope that enough material has been presented below so that others can find out other things from our case studies.

But the main body of the research will consist of the description of the case study – what happened, what the informant(s) said about themselves, what they did and why they thought they did it; what they felt and assumed; what the researcher actually saw and heard; and what sense/meaning the researcher makes of this story. This last part is very important. Here we will try to draw upon all our own background experience of other research and also on our reading. We will try to relate what we saw and heard to the wider literature on literacy and numeracy. We will indicate where we saw what we believe to be a good example of something which is described in the literature or where the story we are telling challenges commonly held assumptions.

We are not preparing a scientific thesis but telling a story. The important point is to try to tell our story to someone else so that they can understand what we are saying. Just like the turtle and the fish.

In doing this, we will need to extract from our case studies detailed accounts of the actual process being studied, including the voice of the participants. We must keep our own voice to a minimum. But equally we cannot and should not try to hide ourselves. We need to recognise the role that we as researchers have adopted. In every case study, the reader needs to be able to see where the researchers are at any stage of the research. Equally we need to try to identify our own personal biases and assumptions. One evidence of this are those occasions when we find ourselves struck by what appears to us to be unusual or unexpected.

In writing up, an ethnographer will avoid generalisation and personal judgment. The aim is to state what actually happened, not what *generally* happens. Our work is aimed at challenging generalisations: all we can say is that in our case studies certain things happened or were said, not that *all* such people do or say these things.

In writing up, as well as in data collection, it will be necessary for us to try to obtain knowledge from different sources for triangulation purposes. We can check up what some of informants are saying with information from other situations or even from within the same situation. Comparing all our different media (photos, documents, observations, notes and artefacts) will provide triangulation, as will reading other ethnographic studies. Sometimes we will be able to find other informants to explore similar subjects.

In writing up our studies, we should try to avoid adding further difficulties to comprehension for the audience by adding a new terminology too quickly. We should follow the pedagogical rule of starting from the familiar; we can analyse and reflect on our own analyses later.

The workshop agreed on a general format for the reports, although each researcher was encouraged to use a different format if they felt it necessary – the group did not advocate a one-size-fits-all template for such reports. Nevertheless, they felt that each report should include an introduction (short and brief), with background information. It should state the objectives and describe the methodology used.

The main body of the report should describe the findings, the literacy and numeracy practices found in the context and how they were used. It was important that the researcher should not write down everything found, although we recognised that the process of selection of matter related to the objectives is a difficult task. We also felt that the report should avoid negative value judgments, our aim is to try to understand what is being done and why, not to judge it.

A conclusion can be added, drawing out some of the implications of the findings, especially for our teaching and learning programmes for literacy and numeracy. This will always be tentative, for others will see things in our data which we cannot see. And reflection and analysis takes time before we can make use of the ideas in our teaching. This is explored in Part III of this book.

Conclusion

This LETTER programme seeks to introduce the workshop participants to the concepts and practice of ethnography as applied to local literacy and numeracy practices. In part, it was a theoretical study; in part it was practical, for all the participants undertook micro-studies during the workshops and a larger study between the workshops. In this first part of the programme, the participants saw the need for ethnographic studies to be added to their existing ways of finding out about the learners in their learning programmes. They explored some aspects of how to go about such studies and how to write them up. What follows is the series of case studies of local literacy and numeracy practices in Ethiopia which they produced, and then the analysis we drew from these case studies as applied to our adult learning programmes.

Readings

Papen Uta, 2005, *Adult Literacy as Social Practice*, Chapter 4: Using ethnography to study literacy in everyday life and in classrooms, London: Routledge.

Hamilton, M., 2005, 'Understanding the everyday: adult lives, literacies and informal learning', in McKeough, A., Phillips, L., Timmons, V., and Lupart, J. (Eds.). Understanding Literacy Development: A Global View. Newark, NJ: Erlbaum.

Heath, S.B. and Street, B., 2008, *On Ethnography: Approaches to Language and Literacy Research*, National Conference on Research in Language and Literacy; Teachers College Columbia.

Nirantar and ASPBAE, 2007, *Exploring the Everyday*, Delhi.

References

Agar, M., 1996, *The Professional Stranger: an informal introduction to ethnography* 2nd edition. Academic Press: NY. especially new chapter 1 'Ethnography Reconstructed: the Stranger at Fifteen', pp. 1-51.

Argyris, C. and Schon D.A. 1974, *Theory in Practice: increasing professional effectiveness* San Francisco: Jossey Bass.

Atkinson, P. Coffey, A. and Delamont S. 2003, *Key Themes in Qualitative Research – continuities and change* Walnut Creek CA: Altamira Press.

Beins, B.C 2004, *Research Methods: A tool for life* Boston: Allyn and Corbin.

Bryman, A. 2004, *Social Research Methods* Oxford: Oxford University Press.

Burns, R. 2000, *Introduction to Research Methods* Thousand Oaks, CA: Sage.

Clifford, J. 1986, 'Introduction', in Clifford J. and Marcus G.E. (eds) *Writing Culture: The poetics and politics of ethnography* Berkeley: University of California Press.

Coffield, F. 2000, *The Necessity of Informal Learning* Bristol: Policy Press.

Cohen, L., Manion, L., Morrison, K. 2000, *Research Methods in Education* London: Routledge.

Cornwall, A., Musyoki, S., Pratt, G., 2001, *In search of a new impetus: practitioners' reflections on PRA* IDS Working Paper, Brighton: IDS University of Sussex.

Dyson, A. and Genishi, C 2005, *The Case: Approaches to language and literacy research* NCRLL; Teachers College Columbia.

Eraut, M. 2000, Non-formal learning, implicit learning and tacit knowledge in professional work, in Coffield 2000:12-31.

Geertz Clifford, 1988, *Works and Lives: The anthropologist as author* Cambridge: Polity.

Geertz, Clifford, 1973, *The Interpretation of Cultures*, New York, Basic Books.

Green, J. and Bloome, D. 1997, 'Ethnography and ethnographers of and in education: A situated perspective', in Flood, J., Heath, S. and Lapp, D. (eds.), *A handbook of research on teaching literacy through the communicative and visual arts* (pp 181-202) New York, Simon and Shuster Macmillan.

Guijt, I. and Cornwall A. 1995 *Critical reflections on the practice of PRA* Participatory Learning and Action Notes, 24, London: IIED.

Hall B 2006 'Ethnographic methods' http://www.sas.upenn.edu/anthro/CPIA/methods/Ethnography.html

Hammersley, M. and Atkinson P. 1995 *Ethnography: principles in practice* London: Routledge.

Headland, T., 2007 Emic and Etic; point of view and its entailments: web 20.2.07.

Hymes, D. 1996 'Narrative Thinking and Storytelling Rights: a folklorist's clue to a critique of education' in *Ethnography, Linguistics, Narrative Inequality: towards an understanding of voice* Taylor & Francis: London.

Kalman, J. 1999 *Writing on the Plaza: Mediated literacy practices among scribes and clients in Mexico city* Hampton Press: Cresskill NJ.

Kvale S. 1996 *Interviews: An introduction to qualitative research interviewing* London: Sage

Lett, J. 2007 Emic/ Etic Distinctions web 20.2.07

Miles, M.B. and Huberman, A.M 1994, *An Expanded Sourcebook: qualitative data analysis* Thousand Oaks, CA: Sage.

Mitchell, J., 1984, "Typicality and the Case Study" pp. 238-241 in R.F. Ellen (ed.) *Ethnographic Research: a guide to conduct* Academic Press: New York.

Mitchell, J. 1984, "Typicality and the Case Study" pp. 238-241 in R.F. Ellen (ed.) *Ethnographic Research: a guide to conduct* Academic Press: New York.

Moll, L, Amanti C, Neff D. and Gonzalez N. 1992, Funds of knowledge for teaching: using a qualitative approach to connect homes and classrooms, *Theory into Practice* 31.2: 3-9.

Polyani, M. 1966, *The Tacit Dimension* New York: Doubleday.

Prinsloo, M. and Breier, M. 1996, *The Social Uses of Literacy* Amsterdam: Benjamins/Sacched.

Punch, J. 1998, *Introduction to Social Research*, Sage

Reber A 1993 *Implicit Learning and Tacit Knowledge* New York: Oxford University Press.

Straka G A 2004 Informal learning: concepts, antagonisms and questions www.itb.uni-bremen.de accessed 2 January 2006.

Street, B.V. 1984, *Literacy in Theory and Practice* Cambridge: Cambridge University Press.

Tacchi, J., Slater D., Hearn, G. 2003, *Ethnographic Action Research* New Delhi: UNESCO.

Todorov, T. 1988, "Knowledge in Social Anthropology: distancing and universality", Anthropology Today, vol. 4, no. 2.

Uddin Md Aftab 2005 'Perceptions, learning and uses of literacies in relation to livelihoods: A case study of two Bangladeshi villages', unpublished PhD thesis, University of Nottingham.

Wilkinson, S. and Kitzinger C. 1995, *Feminisim and Discourse* Thousand Oaks, CA : Sage.

Yin, 1994, *Case study research: design and method* Beverley Hills, CA: Sage.

Yin, R. 1989, *Case study research design and methods* Newbury Parl, CA: Sage.

2
Literacy and Numeracy in Livelihoods

These case studies of local literacy and numeracy practices in Ethiopia relate to several different aspects of daily life. The first set are devoted to livelihoods, especially incomes and expenditure. Here the counting systems adopted by many non-literate persons are very different from those taught in the (adult) classroom.

CASE STUDY 1A
Women in Small Scale Business in Arbaminch Town

This case study is drawn from the members of a micro-credit scheme. It was conducted by Kebede Jobir and colleagues from Arbaminch College of Teacher Education.

Introduction
Generating and controlling income enables women to learn to handle cash and, by managing their micro-enterprise, to learn how to handle the family budget and manage debt. This allows them to assert their viewpoint on family decision making and to take certain decisions alone.

Arbaminch town is located in the Southern region, about 505 kms away from the capital of Ethiopia (Addis Ababa). It is the centre of Gamo Gofa administrative zone. Being located near two rift valley lakes Abaya and Chamo, and bounded by Nechsar National Park, the town serves as a centre of tourist attraction and for running small scale business activities.

Methods and Process

This research used ethnographic case study methodology, which should not be confused with other kinds of case studies, such as those used as exemplars of good practice. Thus the methods used were:

- Identifying the individual women who take loans by asking the nearby Arbaminch microfinance office
- Focused observation
- Informal interview
- Observation while walking to the office and individual houses with informants
- Visual ethnography including photography.

Small Group Focused Discussion

We talked to a small group of nine women from the areas of *Limat, Konso* and *Menoriasefer* all of whom were members of a micro-credit scheme. They all said that they were not born in these areas but had come in from the countryside to get work and money. Where they came from, there was *"only farming"*[1]. One of them said,

> "I hate it, because my parents were farmers but they don't have money and they didn't even send me to school, they are poor; I don't want to live their form of living. So I got information from one of my friends Kantuse who went to Arbaminch before me and asked her to take me to the town, with no information to my family, because they refused to allow me to go away. I came to Arbaminch and with the help of Kantuse we got work as house maids. Then both of us got married". We asked Kantuse whether she can read and write. She said she had learned "in school up to grade 4, while I lived with my parents. My parents didn't want me to continue, because they want me to work in their farm, so I dropped out and came to town. I was married and now I raise my family. If I get a chance, I want to work as a cleaner or otherwise I want to work in a Arbaminch textile factory.

During this focus group discussion, we asked the women how they hoped to improve their lives and their family lives. They said,

"We have dreams of improving our families' economic well-being, developing our own income-generating project, setting our children, especially our daughters, on a path to a better life through school and even university which they never dreamed of for themselves". We asked the elderly spokeswoman Hambelle, "Why do you focus on your daughter?" "Because I don't want her to live my life. It is bad, I don't have a better home, clothes, and my way of life is not good. We are poor. I was even beaten by my drunken husband. I used to take a loan from the microfinance and struggle to raise my family, make my children to go to school, even buy trousers for my husband but he makes me angry, all to make that devil, his secret wife, happy. My friends laugh at me, they told me what he buys for her, everybody knows. She gave him a child, cheated him, and he gave our money for her", and her eyes filled with tears.

Despite all these difficulties, the interviewed women responded that they have no choice but to act, and inspired by their dreams try to overcome the obstacles in their path in order to supplement the inadequate incomes their husbands bring in, when it is not enough to provide all the family's income. For this, they said that they talk with their family, friends and neighbours and act on their strategies individually or in a co-operative manner.

CASE STUDY 1B

A Co-operative Business: Hambelle and Guye

Hambelle with her friend Guye work cooperatively; they are also neighbours. We talked to them, and they said,

"We take a loan of 500birr each. Our children in school write the loan and the income on separate sheets of paper. We keep this secretly, because it may get mixed with other papers and be lost. We have different activities like araki making, tella, buying clothes, and retailing, etc., because if one fails to be profitable, the others will compensate; for example, if banana retailing costs decrease, we get income from araki or others. We got this knowledge from our friend Gelete who said during the coffee ceremony that earlier she used to sell one item, making alcoholic drinks only, and had few consumers, didn't know her profit, and failed to return her loan on time, so she was not allowed the next round of money. So her experience helped for our success. Because we got experience of different items, we know the market needs, and thus we shift from one item to another based on the consumers' need."

In addition to this, both women said that

"we have some form of enterprise which is not known by our family and is not documented. It is banana trade as distributor, buying from farmers and retailing to small-scale street traders". 'Why do you hide this information from your families?' Both laughed and said, "If it is known by our husbands, they will be suspicious. Husbands need to control and decide on all the family's income, they don't want us to buy and wear good clothes and shoes, they want us to serve him and our family only, so it is to fulfil our need; and also it serves as a guarantee. You see in our society, the husband is dominant, due to different reasons. If he wants to marry another, he chases us out of our family and gets married to another. So if such a thing happens, we may struggle with this little hidden money. Thus we hide the information for a guarantee, and also to help us to look beautiful to our husband, so that he does not marry others", and they laughed. They continued, "To this trade, we contribute 23 birr each, with a capital of 46 birr. We chose this number because it is the day of St. George's church where we pray every month. This is the core for our secrecy to one another in the name of him, St. George's church. We go to the church, hold its door and promise in the name of him to be honest with one another and keep our secret. The whole money that we collect from our sales was kept in a locked box with St.George's picture on it and kept in her [Hambelle's] house". 'Why was the St.George's picture kept on the box?' Because if somebody tries to steal our money, St.George will defend and punish him/her". The church is not more than 100 metres from their homes.

We asked, 'When did you start this trading? Is it profitable? How do you calculate your profit?' They said,

"We started to work together in October 2006. It is profitable because we shared out our original sum with a profit of 75birr and 35 cents for each of us after one year. We didn't use any calculation because we put the money we get from selling with no mixing with other money, because it is the money that we promise to one another in the name of St George's church not to mix, not to buy anything from it or lend it to others etc, so we collect it in a locked box for a year and we open it at the day of St.George i.e. 23rd of the month. Because this is the date in which we believe in him, we are honest with our share and sales, we believe that we remove any dishonest action especially on this date. This year we increased our capital by doubling the initial money (46 birr each) to make a total 92 birr. We will continue this activity by increasing the same amount of money we contributed, bearing in mind the day of the angel St. George".

Hambelle and Guye banana selling

Hambelle and Guye carrying bananas to the market

CASE STUDY 1C
Guyato, A Trader of Konsosefer

One of the respondents, Guyato Guyala, lives in Konsosefer; her house is a little bit far from the centre of the town. We talked to her and she said, "I used the age of my elder daughter 16 years for 1600 birr (one thousand six hundred birr) to know the total amount of money that I borrowed from the microfinance last year. I used her age, because I never forget her age of 16 because it was at this age that she dropped out of school when her father was out of government work and become unemployed. We didn't have enough money, her father was always angry, not happy, drunken; he beat me always. In this condition, my friend Kumee shared her experience and told me to take a loan from microfinance. I discussed this with my daughter and she decided to leave the school until the family situation was changed, and I agreed and she helps me now in boiling cheka" (a cultural drink of Konso).

Literacy and Numeracy in Livelihoods 45

Guyato boiling *cheka*

Guyato's daughter boiling *cheka*

Guyato said that her family condition was now good. "We get money by selling cheka, and retailing of sheep, so it is good". I asked how she calculated her profit. She responded that "a cup of cheka sells at 0.40 cents, and out of the 50 kilo grain that I bought, I got about 70 to 80 cups; the profit of which is nearly 28 birr. I know the amount of profit based on the water that I add to the boiling container by assuming losses by evaporation.

Guyato also used to buy a sheep at a low cost, feed it from the product of the *cheka* and sold it at a high price. 'How do you know about buying and retailing of sheep?', we asked. She said, "During the coffee ceremony with my neighbours, we talk about marketing. One day, a woman, Gadisse, told me her experience in buying sheep at a low cost, feeding it from the product of cheka and retailing. We pray in the same church and she has never told me things that hurt my family, I believed her. I buy small sheep at a low cost, my daughter writes how much money I spent, and during retailing I ask my daughter to read for me the amount of money I paid previously to know the amount of profit money that I get from retailing of the sheep."

Sign of *cheka* **and Guyato's sheep**

I asked Guyato when and how she used to return her loan. Guyato answered as follows: "I used to pay monthly 40 birr for a period of 40 months; for this I counted 40 grains (of maize) and kept it in safe place, in which a single grain represents 40birr, so when I pay 40 birr, I reduce one grain and so on". 'From where did you get such experience?' She said, "I heard when my father Guyala talked about his father i.e. my grandfather who was dead before my birth. My father talked to our family about my grandfather. I heard my father say that his father was having so many sheep, he used sand to count their number; when there is a new birth, he added one sand grain; if he slaughtered, he reduced one sand grain and so on. I was astonished by the knowledge of my grandfather at that time when I heard his practice, so I think it is my grandfather's experience that was transferred to me and helps me to calculate my loan of return." During our observation, we saw that there were 26 grains. When we asked how many had been paid and how many remained, she automatically responded, "I have paid 560 birr, and 1040 remain", which is correct.

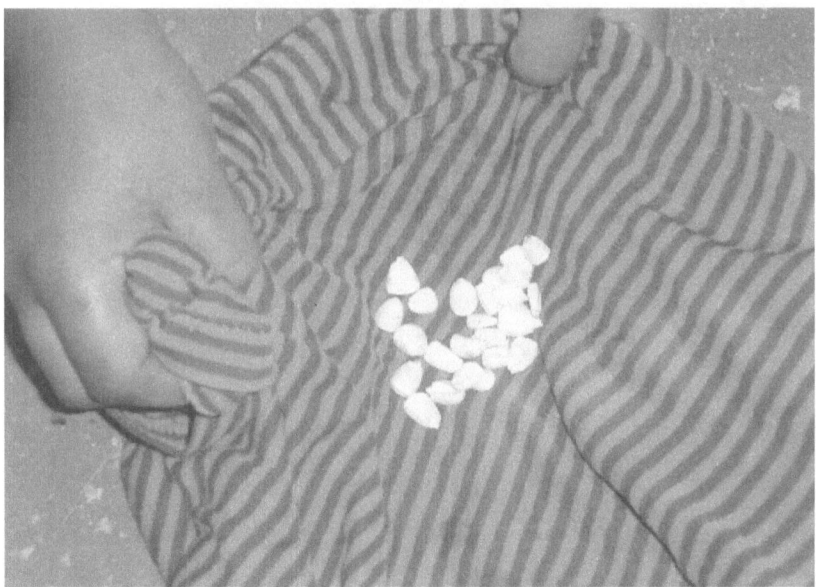

A single grain represents 40 birr

I asked Guyato, 'Do your family members know where you keep this grain?' "No", she said, "Because my husband always asks me for money to buy drink. I refuse to give and he gets angry and we quarrel always. He thinks I have more money and, he used to say, he is unemployed, so I am afraid that if he knows this, he may steal and throw away my grains to make me angry", she said. I asked her, 'What if something happens to you when you are away from home? Or if something like fire burns your house?' She smiled and "Don't worry", she said, "I am not a mother who leaves problems to my family. Every information about this is known by my mother. I told her and she knows; I also keep some money in her home, because I am afraid of my husband that he may steal it when I am not at home."

Wudnesh marketing

Wudnesh in the market: A different attitude towards microfinance

The microfinance responsible person, Negash Getachew, informed us that they are helpful and work to enhance the women's empowerment, and in doing so they are successful in achieving their goals. This is their view, but not that of all the users.

For example: One of the informants in the market, Wudnesh, told us she hated microfinance, because after she had taken a loan of 600 birr earlier, due to lack of experience, she misused the money and could not return her loan. She said, "I asked them, saying, 'I am illiterate, you are the government, hence excuse me or give me a longer time', but they refused and I sold my cow from which I earn 65 birr from a litre of milk. After this, I have been preparing pepper, buying and retailing common salt, etc. They are not good, they didn't help us, there is no training, no follow-up, but simply collecting the money, with no excuse. I hate them." 'How did you misuse your first loan?' we asked. She said, "They gave us the money and said, 'All of you work with this money and return it after a long time'; so I was happy and took the money, and used it for different activities that I can't remember now." 'But you know that it is the government money and you should have to return it?' "Yes", she said and added, "There is no clear information on how and when to return it, but they used us for their propaganda".

From this case study one can understand that every adults have their own local literacy and numeracy practices, thus further study is needed on how many profit does the banana resellers obtains and how much does the local drink residue that the sheep feed costs?

[1] We have translated their words from Amharic into English.

CASE STUDY 2
Tirhas: A small Scale Business in Adwa, Tigray

This case study has been prepared by Sisay Kahsay. It describes a group of ten women who run a small scale shop near a college of education, each member taking two days in turn to serve in the shop.

Introduction

This case study was conducted in Ethiopia, region Tigray, town Adwa. It explains how this woman engaged in a small scale business with a group. The purpose of this study is to see her literacy and numeracy practices as well as the ways of accomplishing her daily activities.

It was 23 October 2007 when I walked from my home to the market place of Adwa town. I saw different items placed on the market side of the road. Suddenly I met Tirhas, a woman who was my neighbour, selling different items and we exchanged greetings in our local language Tigrigna. Tigrigna is widely spoken in that local area.

I asked the woman, "Are these items prepared for a wedding ceremony?", "*Yes,*" she replied showing a smiling face and laughing. Again I asked her, "Why are you laughing?" She said, "*I told you that for joking. These items are prepared for selling; it is our small scale business shop.*" I decided to try to assess how they buy and how they sell without her knowledge by chatting with her.

Another day I went to Tirhas and I tried to observe without her knowledge. I asked about the prices of the items. She asked me, *"Why are you asking me all these things?"*, so I told her my purpose. The woman accepted my reason and was ready to tell me her story.

Tirhas Gidey lives in Northern Ethiopia, Tigray region, in Adwa town Kebele 07. She is 34 years old. She has two daughters. Their names are Tarik Leul aged 17, she is grade 10, and Selam Leul aged 15, she is in grade 9; both of them are in school. I asked her how she joined this small-scale business and she said, " I was a fighter with TPLF/EPRDF in the field. After the Derg Regime failed, I became a civilian and started leading my life with the salary I got for my retirement. It was very small and I couldn't manage very well with my family. So I sent Helen to her father to Axum, because we were divorced. Due to this economic problem, I decided to discuss with my friends to do something, and we agreed to establish an organisation of a small-scale business in 1989 E.C. To open this small scale business, we had not enough money. So we agreed to apply to the Don Bosco Catholic Church to get support from church. When we went to the church, we got the leader of the Church and we told him our problem. The leader of the church volunteered to help us with 80.00 birr every month.

"However" she said, "It could not be a permanent solution, rather we were developing dependency. Therefore, we changed our idea. That is, to borrow 500.00 birr each, making a total of 5000.00 birr from this church and 500.00 birr each from the small scale business office, total 5000.00 birr; totally we borrowed 10,000.00 birr.

I asked her, "How do you allocate your money to different items and how did you get the shop?" She said, "By the money we got from microfinance and the church, we invested based on the need of the community", because the women's small scale shop is near the teacher training college. "We got the shop by the help of microfinance office. So the students [of the college] need different items such as more barley flour (tihini)". I asked, "Why?" She said, "Because they can drink it simply by stirring it with water. So we invest more money in barley flour than in other items." Moreover she said, "Some of the students need to prepare food by themselves. Therefore, they need pepper. Hence next to barley flour, we invest money in pepper".

I also asked her, "Besides the small plastic packets, you have pepper in quintals, so why do you display it prepared in quintals?" She said, "We have an agreement to supply one quintal of pepper to Adwa Hospital every six months. That is why we make ready the pepper in quintal (100kgs)." I asked her, "Do you have a written agreement?" She said, "No, it is not written but we supply every six months". I asked her to tell me the price of the items. She told me that the price of each item is clearly depicted. They bought different items and prepared different things.

Item	Bought	Selling prices
Pepper	50.00 birr for one kilo	60.00 birr
Lentil	7.5 birr for one kilo	8.00 birr
Bean	5.50 birr for one kilo	8.00 birr
Macaroni	6.50 birr for one kilo	7.00 birr
Salt	50.00 birr for one quintal	75.00 birr

52   *Everyday Literacies in Africa*

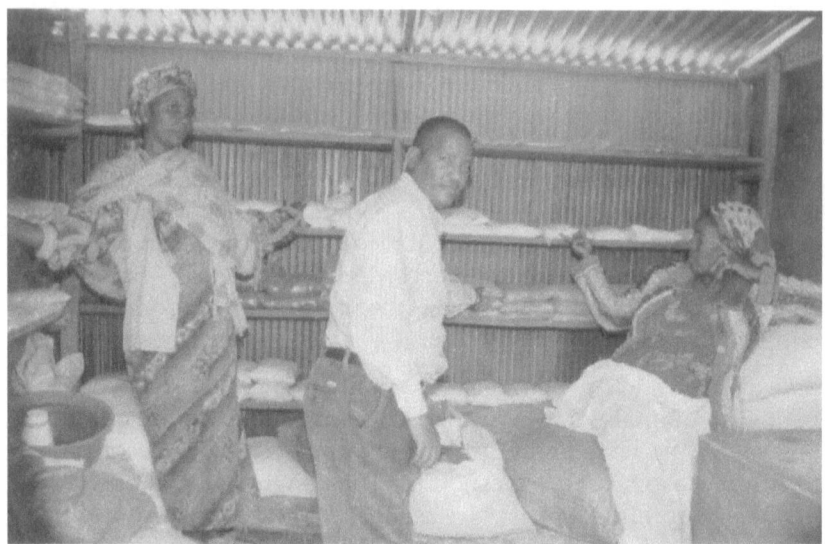

The small-scale shop

I asked her, "Do you have rules within the small scale business shop?" She said, "Yes. For example, if anybody wants to withdraw from small-scale business, she can withdraw at any time. If somebody violates the rules such as corruption, she will be dismissed from the membership."

I was eager to know how she records her expenses and profits. Therefore, I decided to spend two days with Tirhas and her friend in the small-scale business shop. Her friend was not happy with me in spending that much time in the small-scale business shop. I explained my purpose to both of them. But her friend did not accept this and she and I discussed it with Tirhas. Then they told me to bring a letter of permission from the microfinance office. When I wrote my application to the small-scale business office, they gave me a letter of permission. Then after that, they volunteered to give me all the information.

I asked Tirhas, "How do you record your items?" She said, "*Since some of us can write and read, we do not have any problem in recording items. But some of us cannot write and read. However, when we sell different items during the two days of our turn, we have our mechanism, that is, every item is packed in small plastic bags. Therefore, when we transfer to the next turn of our members, we have two alternatives: We should have to transfer the already counted plastic bags; or if we sold different items, we should give the already budgeted money to one of the auditors."

I asked her; "How many members do you have?" She said, "We are ten."

I asked her, "From all these items, how do you calculate your profit?" She said, "I can calculate my profit easily because for each item I know how much I bought and how much I have sold". I understood in that way that from a kilo of pepper, they got 10 birr profit. Her friend also said, "Sometimes we sell some item without profit", and I asked her, "Why?" She said, "For example, we buy bananas for 4 birr and we resell them for 4.00 birr. We do this in order to attract our customers."

While I talk with them, one foreigner, an English speaker, came and he wanted to buy macaroni. They tried to communicate by signs; additionally I helped them by translation. By that case, I became interested to know about their communication with other languages. I asked her, "Do you know any other language other than Tigrigna?" She said, "I try to speak Amharic to some extent. But I do not speak other languages." So I asked her, "If so, how do you communicate with other language speakers, to buy and sell the items?" Tirhas said, "I can communicate by signs and sometimes by mediators."

I also asked her, "Have you had enough time to return your loan? And how much money have you deposited up to now? Where do you put it?" She said, "Yes, we have had enough time to return our credit, that is 500.00 for Catholic Church and 500.00 for small scale business office every month, and we have returned all. We have 40,000.00 birr and we put it in the bank." I also asked her, "Do you put the money in the bank all the time?" She replied, "We share some amount of money during celebrations and festivals during New Year and Christmas, for instance."

While I was discussing with Tirhas, her daughter Tarik, who is 17 and attending school came and gave her some money. I asked her, "Why did your daughter give you money? From where did she bring it?" She said, "She works one shift as a cleaner at Don Bosco, her salary is 20 .00birr per week and I collect her money. When she gives me the money every week, she puts her signature, to assure that she gave me the money. By now she has collected 640.00 birr."

CASE STUDY 3
Literacy and Numeracy in Life's Histories – Small Scale Industry

Literacy and Numeracy in Livelihoods: Asha, the Weaver

> Literacy and numeracy are not only used in the community when trading; it is also embedded within many crafts and industries run on a small scale in rural and urban areas of Ethiopia. This case study concerns a weaver.Compiled by Markos Mekuria, Lecturer and Adult Education Coordinator, Awassa College of Teacher Education

This study was conducted in Southern Ethiopia, Awassa which is about 270 kms from Addis Ababa. It illustrates the case of one individual who is engaged in weaving business. As the study adopted an ethnographic approach, the researcher tried to learn and understand many issues from the practices in the study. The research methods employed in this study were interview, informal discussions, observation and visual documentation (photos) of the selected activities. Photographing and interviews were done with the permission of the subject of the study.

It was Saturday morning 16 January 2008. I went to the Saturday market to buy a *'Gabi'* (a cultural cloth made of cotton, used to wear during cold time) for my father. There I met a *'Gabi'* seller and bought one *'Gabi'* by 160 birr. I was struck by his interesting speech and the way he sought to attract the attention of *'Gabi'* buyers, and I became very interested to know something about this man and his occupation. I politely asked him whether or not he would be willing to tell me his name and his background . He replied positively, and said, "*My Name is Asha Agena. I live in Awassa. I was born and brought up in Awassa, Berhan village, the son of a weaver and farmer. I used to help my father while he was weaving. I learned weaving skills from him. After his death, I continued weaving in order to help my mother, my two brothers and my sister, for I was the elder son in the family.*"

Then I asked him whether he had schooling or not. He replied, "I had no schooling. I did not go to any school, my father did not send me to any school, for he was non-literate and wanted my labour at that time." Asha continued saying, "This reminds me of something. You know , when I grew older, I decided to get married and be blessed with children . After eight years, I got married and currently I am the father of three kids. I started sending my kids to school. This year I sent my daughter to one of the private schools, she is learning at grade 1 and my son to the kindergarten level one, to take revenge against my no schooling."

After that, I told him that I would be interested to know more about himself and his occupation another time by visiting his home. After that, we made an appointment by exchanging addresses and I departed. We met on Tuesday May 6, 2008 as per our prior appointment. After exchanging greetings, I started asking how he makes cultural clothes such as 'Gabi,' 'Kutta,' and ' Netela,'. He answered, "First, I buy a medeb (set of raw cotton) of cotton from the market, (Gabi) and give it to my wife for processing it and she converts the cotton into thread (mag) form in her free time, including the night time. And then she or myself convert the 'likakit' (mag) into 'Kesem' (a small cut bamboo which contains cotton thread on it). For example, he said, currently the price of one medeb of cotton in the market is 20 birr and that amount is adequate for making one 'Gabi' or 'Kutta' (another form of flat cultural cloth used to wear during cold time)." He added, " I use 'Kesem' or Likakit' to determine the amount of mag adequate for one 'Gabi' or 'kutta' . To make one ' Gabi' or 'Kutta', about 60 medium size 'likakit' of mag are adequate. I convert the mag (or likakit) into 'kesem' form, for it is more convenient to throw or use between the stretched threads."

Asha (the weaver) also informed me that one medium size 'likakit' of mag can be converted into three 'kesems', and to make one 'Gabi' or 'Kutta', about 210 'kesems' of cotton thread are enough.

Suddenly I asked, "How do you know this?" He answered, "From my experience. I know it in two ways. First I calculate it in my mind and secondly by counting my fingers, that is, representing one finger for three 'kesems' or for one' likakit'." I was also interested to learn the differences between 'Gabi', 'Kutta' and 'Netela'. I asked him, "Are there any differences and similarities among 'Gabi' ,'Kutta ' and 'Netala' ?" He replied, "'Gabi' and 'Kutta' are similar in many things except their length. 'Gabi' is two arm lengths longer than 'Kutta'. They are made from similar materials. However, 'Netela' and 'Gabi' are different. 'Netela' is made from 'dir' (white factory-made thread) only. It is called 'dir' be 'dir' and has embroidery at the two end parts of its length. However, 'Gabi' and 'Kutta' are made from 'mag' (the locally processed cotton) and' dir'. It is said to be 'dir' be 'mag' and has embroidery at the two end parts of its length. 'Kutta' and 'Netela' can have similar lengths, i.e. five 'kind' (five arm lengths) in length and three' kind' (three arm lengths) in width. 'Gabi' and 'Kutta' are meant for men, while 'Netela' is meant for women and girls."

I asked, "What units do you use to measure their length and width?" He answered, "I use 'kind', 'sinzir' and' ermija' to measure their length and width for making these clothes. I use 'ermija' (a foot step) when stretching' dir' (thread) outside the work station and to fix my local machine in the work station. 'Sinzir' is from the tip of the thumb to the tip of the middle finger when stretched. I also use 'sinzer' to mean half of a 'kind' or two 'sinzir' equal one 'kind'."

I asked, "How long does it take you to make a 'Gabi', Kutta' or 'Netela'?" Asha answered, "Well, it depends on my speed and the type and size of embroidery to be used. For example, it takes me about a day to make a 'Gabi' or 'Kutta', but I can make at least three 'Netelas' in a day." In addition, he told me that the design and the size of embroidery is determined by the preference of the individuals who give orders for the work, although sometimes it is determined by the weaver himself based on the customer's/ retailer's need or market preference.

During my field visit (observation), I observed a work station and asked, "Who established the work station, the machines and other required materials?" He answered, "Most of them were produced by me, but I bought some materials from the shop, I established the work station, the 'dir' and 'mag' processor, the ' kesem'. But other things were bought from the market ." I asked, "How do you protect these tiny cotton threads from being cut during stretching?" He replied, "Before stretching the 'dir' , I prepare the solution of water, sugar, bread and used carbon papers and put the thread into that solution to keep the 'dir' from being broken or cut while stretching. This is a practice which I acquired from my father."

I asked him for whom he makes these clothes, how often he makes them and who helps him. Asha answered, "I make these materials mainly for two people. First, I make 'Gabi' or 'Kutta' or 'Netela' by order for individuals who want to have such a cloth , when they bring all the necessary materials (dir, mag, and coloured threads for the embroidery). For making 'Gabi' or 'Kutta', I charge them 50 birr for each, and for making 'Netela', I *charge them each 20 birr only. Secondly, I make these clothes for sale in the market, especially for retailers. The estimation of materials needed for one 'Gabi' or 'Kutta' is 60 medium size or 40 big size 'likakit' (mag), 8 sets of 'dir', and 8 sets of small balls of factory-made threads of different colours for embroidery are used. And for making 'Netela', three sets of 'dir' which cost 8 birr each and coloured factory-made thread (for embroidery) of 10 birr are needed."*

During discussion, he also told me that his estimation regarding the amount of materials needed was most of the time correct or exact. He also indicated that he has a third option for whom he makes these clothes. He said , " I have a third option, for example, if I finish or complete the work that I was ordered by individuals and by customers (retailers), I will not sit idle; rather I make some of these items for the market , i.e. , for selling them myself in the Saturday market. I sell 'Netela' for 50 to 60 birr, 'Gabi' for 150 to 160 birr and 'Kutta' for 140 to 150 birr when I sell them myself. But if I am busy with duties, I give them to my relative to sell them. I pay him an allowance of 20 birr per day, and in addition I allow him to have the money above the minimum price of the cloth, that is, 50 birr for 'Netela' , 150 birr for 'Gabi' and 140 birr for 'Kutta'."

He went on, saying in his own words that, " Usually I am busy in winter months from Meskerem (September) to Miazia (April) because it is in these months that most of my customers get money and time to give orders. However in the other months, mostly I make on the on-and-off basis and I get some rest." Asha also informed me that he was mostly assisted by his wife. She helps him in buying cotton or 'mag' and 'dir', and in processing and converting these into 'likakit' form and then into 'kesem,' form, in putting and taking out 'dir' from a solution prepared for strengthening the 'dir'. In addition, Asha said, "When my wife is busy and engaged in household and other duties, I used to buy the processed 'likakit' of 'mag' from the market and make the aforementioned clothes." I asked, "How do you determine the quality of your clothes?"

He answered, *"The quality of the produced clothes or materials (Gabi, Ku*tta *or Netela) will largely depend on the quality and type of raw materials used ('mag', embroidery, 'dir', etc) ."*

I asked, "How do you know your profit or loss?" He answered, "I know my profit. I don't do any thing without profit . From a 'Gabi' or

'Kutta', most of the time I get 50 birr profit, when I produce them for individual users and customers. I get more when I sell them myself in the market. For example, as I have informed you earlier, if I buy one medeb of cotton with 20 birr to process it and convert it into 'likakit' (mag), for embroidery 15 birr and for buying eight sets of 'dir' which cost 8 birr each, the total expense will estimated to be about 100 birr, and the price of one 'Gabi' or 'Kutta' is from 150-160 birr, that is why I said, my profit is from 50 to 60 birr per 'Gabi.' For 'Kutta', since it has a length of five 'kinds' (arm length) which is two 'kinds' less than that of 'Gabi', its price will also be less than the price of a 'Gabi' . However, he said, I expect the same amount of profit, i.e. the profit I get from a 'Kutta' will not be less than the profit I get from a 'Gabi'. I invest an equal amount of time. From one 'Netela', I can get about 20 birr." So, as he informed me and illustrated with examples, he is able to estimate the profit he is supposed to get . Asha also affirmed that he knows his expenditure items. He mentioned these items in his own words." I expend my money on food, clothes, school fees and uniforms for my kids, for water, electricity and telephone services for buying cotton (mag), for social services like 'Idir' ,'Mahber' and other expenses.

Finally I asked him how he keeps his money. He replied, " I don't want to keep my money in the Bank, but I save some of my extra money in 'Equb' (a local saving institution). I save 500 birr per month in 'Equb', and I save the rest of my money at my home in different places, which I do not want to tell the exact location." He further informed me that he has his own house and has some amount of reserve money which he is not willing to tell the exact amount.

From this case study, it can be concluded that Asha (the weaver) experiences and has many numeracy practices in his occupation and manages his business without formal literacy.

CASE STUDY 4
Literacy and Numeracy in the Marketplace

The next set of case studies relate to trading in the market place. Here the local ways of measuring are again very different from the standardised approaches of the (adult) classroom.

Literacy and Numeracy in the Marketplace: Ade Yeshi Heyi, a grain retailer

This case study was prepared by Zewdu Deriba, ODA's NFE co-ordinator

This case study has been conducted in market area of kebele 04, Asella town, Oromia regional state, 175 kms south of Addis Ababa. I decided to visit this market regularly with the aim of getting anything pertaining to literacy and/or numeracy as social practices. Although there were many women engaged in business activities, one of the women was able to catch my attention. The name of this woman is Ade Yeshi Heyi.

I visited and observed Ade Yeshi for five days at the market area where she retails grain. I observed that she uses a container locally known as *kuchibelu*, to measure the grain when buying and reselling.

Ade Yeshi told me that she lives with her daughter Meseret Abera in Asella town kebele 06 and is leading a hand-to-mouth life. I guess she is about 60 years old. She says that she cannot read and write, but she can count. For the last 16 years, she has led her life by making and selling local drinks '*arake*' and '*tela*' in her small house. But, as she told me, because she lost money repeatedly in making this local drink; she decided to give up this work. After thinking thoroughly, she went to market to observe the work her relatives do. Her relatives buy different kinds of grains from the farmers or wholesalers and resell to consumers. Observing this, after a week she decided to start this work specialising a little bit. Ade Yeshi buys different kinds of grains as her relatives do. But she mixes them. After mixing, she sells using the same measurement that she uses for buying.

When she buys and resells, while counting cups or *kuchibelus* of grains, no written calculation is used to know the payment. If both the buyer and seller agree to pay 8 birr for 9 cups of grain, she counts

9 cups and says '8 birr'. For a second purchase, she counts from one to nine and says 16 birr (8+8). Also if additional cups of grains needed, she counts again from one to nine and says 24 birr (8+8+8) for herself, using her language, Afan Oromo. The same is repeated for any other additional 8 birr and the buyer pays the amount said during counting.

On my last observation, the fifth day, I tried to discuss with Ade Yeshi to find out how she prepares the grains for selling. Ade Yeshi told me the following, looking at the grains mixed. "I have bought 8 cups of wheat grain for eight birr. Also 12 cups of sorghum for 8 birr differently. Then I mix the two kinds of grains and sell 9 cups of mixed grain for 8 birr for my customers who need it to prepare injera". Also she said, pointing her finger at one bag of grain, "Look at this mixed grain! It is not pure as that of the previous and it is not the mixture of only two kinds of grain. As you see, it is a mixture of maize, barley, wheat and sorghum. I bought 8 cups of wheat and barley for seven birr each and 13 cups of maize and sorghum for 8 birr each. Now I am ready to sell 9 cups of this mixed grain for seven birr for my customers who need it to prepare the local drinks 'arake' and 'tela'."

After her explanation, I asked her, "How do you know your profit?" She answered that it is very easy. "Concerning the sorghum and wheat grain, I bought 8 cups of wheat for 8 birr and 12 cups of sorghum for the same birr. And I sell 9 cups of the two mixtures for birr 8. This means I have a loss of one cup from wheat and gain of three cups from sorghum. That means from the two mixtures of grains, I have a gain of two cups"

"Concerning the other four kinds of grains, I sell 9 cups of the mixtures for seven birr. This means I have a gain of four cups from each of the maize and sorghum, and a loss of one cup from each of the wheat and barley. This shows that I have a profit of three cups from the sale of the mixtures".

After all this, she has told me that though this is not a good profit, both Ade Yeshi and her daughter Meseret have been covering their expenses of daily food and clothing each year since doing this work. Not only this, after her all necessary expenses she saves 2-5 birr or above each week. She does this after counting the principal of 1200 birr that she has borrowed from the credit and saving share company of Oromia. Out of this saving, she saves 21 birr every month at the company she borrowed from.

Lastly I asked her, "For what purpose do you save?" She answered that *"Sometimes I might buy the grains at an expensive cost and before I finish reselling, the cost may fall. During this time I face a loss and these savings will cover this loss".*

From this study I can conclude that:

- being literate (to read and write) is not mandatory to engage in an occupation people want to do and that they can still calculate their profit.
- using a standard unit is not mandatory for buying and reselling purpose.

So I suggest that those who want to prepare teaching materials for the purpose of adult education could examine such calculating practices deeply.

CASE STUDY 5

Three Traders in Aleltu Market in Cheese and Butter, Meat and Grain

After attending the LETTER training, a team of five trainees went out to do ethnographic research using case study approach to gather information on the existing funds of knowledge and to explore the existing literacy and numeracy practices that would assist in developing themes that would reinforce the learning process of adults. With this in mind, the team travelled to the north eastern part of Addis Ababa to Aleltu district and compiled three case studies. The team members were Abraru Sherif, Makda Getachew, Selamawit Admassu, Yared Anthonious and Minna Addisu.

General introduction

Berhe Alleltu *woreda* (district) is located at a distance of 55 kms north east of Addis Ababa with a population of 200,000. A majority of the people are followers of the Christian religion.

Aleltu is a highland area and most of the communities are engaged in subsistence farming. In the market of Aleltu, people from different corners meet to buy and sell. The market is open every Thursday and Saturday, and is estimated to accommodate (according to our observation) about 1000 marketers during its peak hours from 9:30am to 1:30pm.

The research team from Addis Ababa arrived in to Aleltu district on March 1, 2008 to work on their case studies. The team used the following methodologies: observation, dialogue, interview, transect walk, interpreter/mediators, visual ethnography (photography) and on-the-spot analysis.

The case of Efe Alemu, a butter and cheese seller

This case study is based on two interviews with Efe Alemu, a market trader, which took place on November 10th, 2007 and February 29th, 2008 in the Aleltu Saturday market.

Market day is, to many people, not only a market day; for some, it is the day they meet their relatives and friends. It is also a good opportunity for most to exchange information, as some come from adjacent districts. It is also an interesting spot for the youth to choose their mate. Observing the different scenarios taking place in the market, the market seems to operate in its own unique ways. It holds its shape, and sellers of similar items sit together displaying what they have to the buyers. All seem to have their own style to attract the buyers. The sellers in the market appear to be competing with each other, but giving more weight to the formal and informal relationships with each other, they try to attract buyers mostly by their eye contacts.

Literacy and Numeracy in Livelihoods 63

Efe Alemu at her stall

Among the different sellers in this market, Efe Alemu is one. Around 9:30am, Efe was making herself comfortable sitting close to her selling place "*Medeb*" (the name of her stall), preparing and re-arranging, re-organising what she brought, negotiating, greeting people she knows, etc. On that very busy marketday, she was actively trying to attract her customers in a better fashion than her other counterparts were doing, which at the same time attracted the attention of the team. Efe has counted years since she started selling butter and cheese in this same market. Efe, with her villagers travel about three to four hours to reach the market twice every week.

Efe was born in the rural town of Berhe where she lives now[1]. Her parents have given birth to seven children (four boys and three girls). Efe is the sixth child of her parents. In her childhood, she was occupied with assisting her parents with household chores and tending the cattle. Efe got married at the age of 17, although girls in her tradition get married at an earlier age of say 13. We asked her how she knew her exact age of marriage, because we know that a birth certificate is not a common practice, especially in rural areas. She said that it was

---

1   The interviews were conducted in Amharic and Oromifiya

looking at the record kept by the local church elite which helped her to know her age. A priest who is close to the family members told her her age (we think this needs further investigation in the field). In the Ethiopian Orthodox Church, every day of the month is made into a religious day, and she said that this helped her to know the dates and the months. She began naming the days by 'St Abo' which is the 5th day of a month, and a week from 'Abo' is St Michael, 12th day of the month. St Gabriel is one week following St Michael which is the 19th, then two days later is St. Mary, the 21st. Two days later is St George, the 23rd. This is how she counts the dates in a month. When she was asked about her age, it took her only a few seconds to tell her age, and *"I am now left with a year to be fifty"* was how Efe told us her age.

Efe had had no chance of going to school, having been born of parents who had not gone into any kind of formal education but who have amazing skill of counting numbers, which she learned from her parents using beans, dried sheep waste called *'betet'* and using her fingers. She starts counting first using her hand fingers, then her toes, and if the counting goes on, she uses beans (if available) or dried sheep waste. *"It is easy. I use my fingers and if the counting continues, I will collect grains of beans; otherwise I use sheep 'betet' (sheep waste) ... Tens of hundreds equals one thousand"*.

During her childhood when she was a cattle herder, it was not only by counting that Efe identified her cattle but also by their names: *"'lomi', 'bure', 'boka', 'gura', 'dale',...are some of my cattle I went after"* Efe told us.

A new chapter in her life started after she was abducted (she was kidnapped by the husband and taken away to his family's home) and married to her husband in a traditional way. In order to formalise the marriage and secure the blessing of her family, the groom bought a dowry of *'buluko'* (a traditional blanket made of cotton) for the bride's father, a dress and *'gabi'* (a traditional shawl made of cotton) for the mother. For the bride, the groom bought perfume, hair oil, an umbrella, jewelry, etc. Efe's family provided a traditional Ethiopian table *'mesob'*, ladle, box for clothing, tray, coffee, soap, sugar, etc in the form of gifts to their daughter and the groom. (It is a tradition to give gifts and different items to the newly married couple but the gifts vary depending on the financial capacity of the family). The whole marriage process and the marriage feast consumed the meagre resources the groom had accumulated so far, as a result of which the married couple were forced to work hard and earn money to sustain their life, as well as support the in-laws. The husband started work in a distant village farming for the rich landlords as a daily labourer. In the same way, Efe also started working in her village cleaning barns, mowing and any other available work that would earn some income. She later started producing traditional trays - *'sefed'*, (a traditional tray made of dry grass which has flat shape), *'enkib'* (a bowl made out of dry grass with curved edges, of different sizes), and *'agelgil'* (a traditional lunchbox made out of dried grass with a cover) - and selling them to generate income.

Traditional trays made by Efe: Agelgil, Sefed, Enkib

In the course of time, Efe was forced to change this income generation activity into the selling of vegetables, as sitting for long hours to produce the traditional trays coupled with continuous giving birth to 8 children (6 girls and a boy, one died at an early age) caused her to have backache. Efe also compared the profit gained and the time spent to produce the traditional trays and the money gained from the sale of vegetables. *"It takes some days to produce local trays and I get only two birr profit, whereas I get more than two birr profit a day from the selling of vegetables."*

According to Efe, to begin vegetable and cabbage selling is not capital intensive. Before starting this business, Efe took close observation of how the women in the market sell what they have. On the next market day, Efe was in the market with her cabbage and vegetables to do her business. *"A day's observation is enough to do business in the market, anybody can do it",* was how Efe expressed how she started the business in the market. Being in the market also helped Efe to look at other sellers in the market and compare the income she earns with that of the other sellers.

A friend of hers in the market who sells cheese and butter introduced Efe to this business activity. Starting this business was not easy as it required some amount of initial capital, which forced Efe to look for an *'arata'* (a traditional money lender). For the traditional lender to give Efe money, she and her husband needed to undergo a long process of convincing the lender. This is an unwritten law agreed and practised to get a loan from traditional money lenders. With her husband, Efe was supposed to give free labour for the family that will lend them money. This was the initial step Efe went through to sway the lender's family to make a loan. She needed to find a guarantor who would have to make an agreement with the lender. She signed an agreement for the guarantor, that if she failed to pay back in the due period, the guarantor would pay back the loan to the lender and the guarantor would the collateral. Her collateral was a plot of farm land and one eucalyptus tree from their land. They cannot take the loan for more than one month. *"It is not easy to get a loan even for a month"* was how she explained the difficulty of getting a loan from traditional money lenders. This is because traditional money lenders calculate their interest per month.

Once she has bought the butter from a farmer for 34 birr, she will resell it for a different price. She decides to buy the butter from a farmer knowing that she will sell and make a profit. She uses different scoops such as a coffee ceramic cup and a tin cup. She uses her hand

to measure the weight and estimate the price. She knows the weight/measures using her hand and fixes the price accordingly.

She sells a small coffee ceramic cup of butter for 11 birr which weighs ¼ kilo (we checked the weight in a shop). Elsewhere in Aleltu market the price of 1 kilo of *Sheno kibe* [a type of butter] was 44 birr and 11 birr was the exact price for a quarter of a *kibe*. We checked the price from another butter selling shop.

The tin cup '*kibe*' of butter weighs a little more than half a kilo and sells for 28 birr – it therefore earns 2 birr extra. She bought it for 26 birr and sells for 28 birr.

The prices vary according to the season. When the Christmas fasting and Easter fasting are ended (*sifeta*), the price will rise. During the fasting season, the price goes down. She checks the price from suppliers who sell butter to the women and other merchants who buy and store and sell as a wholesaler to the town of Addis Ababa. She checks the price of the market before she buys and fixes her selling price. The diagram below shows her market link.

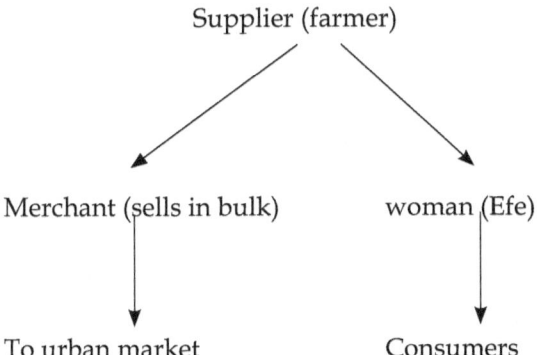

Efe buys from a farmer who supplies butter to merchants who sell in large amounts in the town (through urban markets) and also to small retailers like Efe. She then sells in small amounts to the consumers. So Efe has a way of checking the current price from the supplier (farmer) and fixes her price accordingly.

She uses three different forms of measuring instruments.

No	Units of measurement	Her unit of measurement	
1	Tin cup – 'tasa'	1 tin cup = more than ½ kg	Note here that her estimation for the piled up butter over the cup is measured using her hand as a weighing scale.
2	Bigger size of ceramic cup – 'sini'	4 big cups = 1 kg.	
3	Small size of ceramic cup – 'sini'	5 small cups = 1 kg	
4	Jag – plastic container		

Formerly they used to weigh butter using a tin bowl to buy and resell. Currently all butter sellers use the above listed items for measurement.

In the market, Efe uses different techniques to attract people who come to buy cheese and butter. "I keep the butter and cheese fresh, the bucket and the cups I use are also clean" continued Efe, "The cleanliness of my hand by which I do all the measurement and the exchanges also matters to my customers." She buys cheese and butter from the Onodo market and sells in the Aleltu market on Saturday. If she does not sell all her items, then she will take it to the Hamus Gebayi market. This is how she tries to finish all that she has bought. At other times, Efe buys some items from Aleltu market and sells them in the Hamus Gebayia. On her bad market days, Efe will wrap the butter in castor leaves - 'Gulo leavse', put it in a plastic bag, put it in a basket and hang it up on her wall. She does that to protect it from cats and rats and also from dirt. For her cheese, she will wrap it in a plastic bag and put it in water until she takes it to the market again. She keeps it the same way for about 14 days in cold water but she will not forget to change the water now and then. To give it a pleasant aroma, the cheese and butter will be kept in a smoked container fumigated with fragrant wood-olive (weyra maten) so that the cheese and butter will preserved and it will give it a good taste and flavour.

In buying and selling, Efe repeatedly counts the money before giving change to the customer and vice versa. "Isn't it money?" was what she said when asked about checking her money. "Even if one gives me a 200 birr note, I can give change without any miscalculation." She keeps her money in a traditional wallet and hangs it on her neck under her dress in her chest.

The profit she has made from the sale of her items will be calculated after she has completely traded all she has brought to the market. With her profit, she buys chickens and sells eggs. Her profit covers food items for her family such as coffee, berbere (powdered pepper), onion, salt, oil, etc. She does not sell on credit. "To whom would I sell on credit? I do not know the client. 'I don't sell', I will tell them that I have a problem and won't sell on credit."

At some point in our discussion, Efe was looking at the passersby, so we asked if she wanted to go. "Yes, I have to go at three", Efe responded. We all looked at our watches and it was a quarter to three. We wanted to check how she knows the time and asked her what time it is: "twenty or fifteen minutes is remaining to be nine," responded Efe. It was almost the same time as that of ours. With amazement, we asked her how she knows the time, "I will either ask a person with a watch or I can tell using the shade of my body." Wanting to know more, we followed her into the sun to listen to her explanation. "It is now a few minutes to be 3pm," continued Efe, "as you see, my shadow is shorter than my actual body length; had it been longer than the shade of my body, the time would have been after 3 pm." Efe believes that she is at the same level as an individual who has completed secondary education: "life has given me quite a lot of knowledge; I am no less than a person who has completed secondary education."

CASE STUDY 6

Abate the Butcher Muddles through Life with Multiple Skills

The ethnographer team from Addis Ababa arrived in the town of Berhe in Alleltu woreda on 1 March 2008 to further enrich the case study that was organised two months before. The day was not just any other marketday. Rather, it was two days before the 55 days of the fasting season that is practised among the Ethiopian Orthodox Christians. In these fasting months, the followers are expected to refrain from eating foodstuffs having dairy products, natural protein, egg, meat and chicken. The team was travelling around the market to observe how the market people interact with one another. *"Today, unusually, a lot of people are in this market, as the fasting season is to begin, people want to buy food items and celebrate"*, Beletu told the team. Beletu is a young merchant lady who lives in the town of Berhe and Aleltu, and who has continuously assisted the team in filling communication gaps.

A lot of different kinds of interaction were taking place in the market. Most marketers were with a smiling face as they are safely and peacefully anticipating to start the fasting season. Greetings, bargaining, transactions, negotiations, sounds of different animals, buying and selling of cereals and eggs are among the many things which gave beauty and grace. But the crowd at one end of the market attracted the team most, the butchery market. The team members were observing how the communities interact in the butchery market. The groups of people at the butchery shop look at the pile of displayed meat, discussing among themselves and then with the attendant and finally they leave after paying the price for the meat they chose. In fact, the team were surprised at the way the people were assisted by local and old-hand salespersons of meat so as to manage to choose meat from the piles of meat with a large volume and a good quality and leaving behind other piles of meat. As making observation from afar was difficult, the team decided to come closer, to see and listen to the buyers and sellers of meat at the butchery shop.

As the team members got closer to the butchery shop, they were able to notice two people handling clients coming to this butchery shop. From closer observation, it was understood that meat of different sizes were displayed in groups having different prices. The price of these displayed groups of meat ranged from 100.00 birr to 25.00 birr. Most of the buyers in the market call for the butcher Abate now and then to help choosing the pile of meat they want.

We interviewed Abate and this is what he told us[2].

---

2   This case is compiled in Amharic.

Abate Kebede is a 33-year-old man born in North Shoa, Assageret *woreda*. When Abate was three years of age, his parents sent him to live with his aunt in Berhe *woreda*. While living with his aunt, he had the chance to go to formal school. Abate attended his education up to grade nine. It became very difficult for Abate to continue education after grade nine, as the family was constrained by economic problems. This situation forced Abate, to work as a daily labourer by selling his labour to earn a living.

It was at this time that Abate started working as a daily labourer providing assistance to a local carpenter and a traditional house contractor by carrying and delivering tools to them. His assignment was only on a daily basis, as he did not possess practical experience in the field of carpentry or construction. It took him quite a lot of time and many difficult moments to reach a level of perfection. He says, "I am now one of the most popular and favoured contractors working in this village." Continuing his assertion, Abate explained, "I really want to appreciate those people who have continuously coached, mentored and supervised my construction works and enabled me to be a good constructor of residential as well as business/commercial houses. Once I had constructed/established my own residential home and having proved that I had the required qualities and skills for constructing houses, the near-by communities started requesting me to build their houses, and when the people ask me to build their houses, this has boosted my confidence." Later on, lots of contacts looking for his skills have continued to flow. "I have endured a lot of challenges and lessons in order to reach this level."

Working in the butchery is one of Abate's part-time activities. Abate has been working in a butchery since the time he was admitted into junior secondary school and this part-time work helped him to earn a small income to cover the expenses related to schooling. "Going to a slaughter house, with a neighbour who works there, was also one of my childhood favourite activities that helped me know the quality of meat and a good ox before it is slaughtered." On special days, holidays or when there is high demand for meat, Abate works in a butchery assisting his childhood friend, Pawlose Mehari. Pawlose is the owner of the butchery shop where Abate was working as a part-time assistant.

Abate doesn't use a scale to weigh meat for sale, but he makes a pile of meat in groups (a *'medeb'*) that will cost 100.00 Birr or 50.00 Birr. In this market, the least price of meat that a buyer can get is for 25.00 Birr by dividing the pile of meat for 50.00 Birr into two. *"The community will choose the 'medeb' of meat they want just by looking at the different 'medeb' displayed. The community prefers buying meat by 'medeb' to buying in kilos."* The pace with which other butcheries finish their estimated piles of meat for the clients describes the extents to which other butcheries are performing in the market. *"The number of 'medeb' we are going to prepare will be decided based on the price of the ox and the profit we are expecting to generate out of it."* On that very busy day, Abate is handling all his customers in a very polite and a smiling face.

Abate is confident when he talks about his skills; "having attended the formal education up to grade 9 has helped me, but none of the skills I am currently using are from the schools. All of my works are up to the standard, both in a butchery or and in the field of construction."

CASE STUDY 7
Enani, a Farmer in the Market

Introduction

Our team went into the Aleltu market area and met a woman called Birke. We introduced ourselves and told her why we were there. We asked for her willingness and she agreed to work along with us the whole day. We stayed with her for half a day and agreed to do the remaining interview in her house. We fixed an appointment to meet with her in the afternoon at 11:00 pm at her home. When we arrived at her home, her house was locked. She was not present in her house, so we had to look for her in the village. We found her at her relative's place. We felt she was not interested to continue the discussion. We asked her and she told us that she was not interested. After spending half a day with her, we changed our case and went to Enani's house. The case written below is the story of Enani.

We met Enani when we were looking for Birke. Enani was the one who took us to Birke's relative's house. Enani did not approve of Birke's behaviour and so she took the initiative to be interviewed. The team immediately decided to proceed with Enani as we were running short of time to look for another person and thus we continued our research with Enani's help. Our aim was to get as much information as possible that would help us to compile Enani's case using an ethnographic approach.

Enani – a savings group member

We arrived in Aleltu 'Ilu Farmers' Association' at Enani's residence at about 11:30pm. There were five people in her house with her: her father, sister in law, two nephews and her daughter.

Enani's home

Enani's house is located a few kms outside Aleltu district and 70 metres from the main asphalt road. Their compound covers close to 1,000 sq. metres. Few houses are located in that area; the rest are settled far away. The area's settlement structure is based on family lineage; so the area we visited is owned by Enani's father who gave a plot of land to his daughter to settle there when she got married.

Enani's private hut has one room, separated by a curtain into a living room and bedroom. A radio was on when the team entered the house and the Saturday afternoon Ethiopian radio programme was playing. She has a traditional kitchen built outside the hut 3 metres from the main hut. Next to the kitchen is a small old barn. On the left side, there is an old mud store for animal feed which is also used to keep hens. In the compound there was a dog, a puppy and a number of hens.

Chickens at Enani's house

The living room was neatly arranged with handmade cultural chairs, a table and '*medeb*' (a long seat built all around the wall, made of stone and mud which serves as a chair). The wall was covered with magazine papers and also with some religious, cultural and educative quotations all written in Amharic.

Texts on the wall of Enani's home

Some of the quotations stated:

'Don't admire a person by the type of clothes he/she wears and don't judge a book by its cover' – *'sewen belibsu ena metshafin beshifanu atadinku'*

'Happy Holiday for the Finding of the True Cross' – *'melkam yemeskel baal'*

'People have come to believe in witches and satan rather than believing in one God' *'be-and fetari mamen akitoachu beseytan betenqwai honwal imnetachu'*

'It is neither what you say about yourself nor what people say about you but rather you are the one who knows yourself'. – *'maninethi ante endemitlew ena sewoch endemilut siyhon helinah behak endemiyawkew new'*

Enani prepared the coffee ceremony whereby all family members gathered together. Her husband Bekele came from his farming and joined us. We had dinner of *injera* (local pancake) with fried egg and meat. Then we had our coffee. Her daughter who is five years old also drank coffee with us.

While eating and drinking coffee, we discussed about the food she prepared[3]. We felt that she went out of her way to prepare food and coffee for us. She said, *"I did not buy anything for you. I cooked the eggs and meat I had at home. We drink coffee three times a day, so I had to prepare it for ourselves"*. She got the eggs from her hens. She had bought the meat for her family as it was a time to start the Christian fasting season in two days' time. While drinking coffee, we were all surprised to see her five years old daughter drinking coffee with us like an adult, because children do not usually drink coffee but milk. We make our comment and Enani told us that her daughter started to drink coffee for the sake of tasting the sugar. We observed that Enani's daughter has teeth which are all brown because of decay.

We also discussed about the radio being played. We asked the family members if they play the radio regularly. Enani's father replied, *"We play the radio especially for the educational programme for the children. They learn a lot by listening to the radio."* Enani's daughter and her nephew have not joined formal school yet. *"They are too young to go to school on their own. They can't cross the main road and they will be exposed to a car accident, that is why I did not send my daughter to school this year."* The reason they gave us was the absence of a formal school close by and that it will be hard for young children to walk a long distance at their age. Their parents have a plan to send the children to a formal school in the coming Ethiopian new year, in September 2008.

It was getting dark, so Enani lit a lamp. We then continued our conversation with Enani's father about the radio. We saw there is no electricity, so we asked what power they use for their radio. The father replied, *"We use dry cells."* Our next question was about the cost of dry cells if the radio is played for long hours every day. The father replied, *"It is not that expensive. When the power is low, we take out the dry cell from the radio and charge it on sunlight for long hours. We reuse the dry cell again."* [Actually in our next day's meeting, our camera battery went low and we had to recharge it to take a few extra pictures.]

The other thing we talked was about the tasty *injera* we had. *"I put black wheat together with the 'teff' (cereal used to make injera). That is why it tastes different"*, was Enani's reply.

We decided to continue the interview on the next day. So on the following day, Sunday, we arrived at about 8:45a.m. at her house. There was a monk, her sister in law with her two boys, and Enani's

---

3   This case is compiled in Amharic.

daughter whose name we now learned was Kalkidan. The radio was playing like yesterday.

We asked Enani to tell us her life history in detail.

She was born in the Ilu Farmers Association (the name of a settlement area) with 3 younger brothers and 3 sisters. She went to school up to 8th grade. Her parents always wanted their children to complete their education before settling down. However, the tradition of abduction for marriage would not let Enani continue her education and thus her parents were forced to send her to Debre Zeit (located in the eastern part of Addis Ababa and 110 kms from the village she lived) to live with her uncle. She could not continue her education there probably because she could not produce evidence about her past educational performance. Her uncle in Debre Zeit lived with a relative of her uncle's wife. During her stay in Debre Zeit, she faced the same problem of abduction. She told this to her cousin and also of her interest to go back home. However, the cousin told Enani to stay with her uncle and help him because he lives alone in the house. Enani also missed her family, so she decided to go back home badly. When her father came to visit her, she told him the whole history and insisted to go back home with him. The father became concerned about the seriousness of the problem and decided to take her back home, promising that he and her brother would protect her from an unwanted marriage. *"As long as I am alive, I will protect you in any way I can. Your brother will also be there for you."*

Coming back home, Enani faced the same problem in her village. Due to this, she thought up a strategy to avoid marriage by going to the church and monastery to become a monk. *"My mother brought us through so many hardships and passed away, so I did not want to pass the same process, so I was very much interested to continue my education and live a better life"*. She made her decision believing that people would not chase monks. However, her strategy did not work. She went to Debre Berhan (in the northern part of Ethiopia which is 105 km from her village), in *'Sela Dingay'* , to Tsadkane Marriam church (St. Mary church). There a monk who lives in the monastery told her about her future life, stating that she would be married and would not continue to lead her life as a monk.

Coming back home, Enani started in the grain trade, buying from *Kotu Gebeya* market and *Hamus Gebeya* and reselling in *Aleltu* market which is close by to where she lives. But the trading was not profitable: *"The buying and selling price was not that much attractive and profitable"*. Then she changed her business to brewing and selling a local alcoholic drink called *'arake'*. This was also labour intensive and has a negative effect of changing the face colour and creating freckles. *"It is labour intensive and damages your face colour (melanin)"*.

Enani had to change to brewing another local drink *'tella'* (an alcoholic drink made out of barley) because it is less labour intensive and makes a better profit. Then she started selling the local bread with the *'tella'*. *"My clients told me that if they are served snacks with the 'tella', then they do not need to have breakfast at home and it will save them time to arrive in the market place earlier to start their business"*. The money earned was used to provide for her family (father, sisters and brothers).

Enani was married to a deacon called Bekele on February 23rd, 1995 (EC), which is March 2nd, 2002 GC, which was exactly 5 years before our visit. She was married in a church ceremony. Bekele is a farmer and petty trader. He had been in the grain trade before getting married.

After getting married, Enani moved to the house where we visited her presently. She started making the local drink *'arake'* to sell in Addis Ababa which she was asked to prepare by her sister who lives in Addis Ababa and can sell it at a better price. She produces 10 to 15 litres at a time and sells it for 15 birr per litre.

Currently she is engaged in a number of small business activities such as poultry and sheep farming, and her husband works on cattle fattening. She attended a training programme which gave her an insight to expand her poultry. Enani is a member of a literacy-led savings and credit programme. This programme is funded by PACT and implemented by local non-governmental organisations among which ANFEAE is one. Enani is a member of this programme. She got an opportunity to attend a programme of training among which management committee training was one subject. She was also provided with reading materials that provides information on how to interact in a group, manage group money transactions and businesses, how to be a good leader, etc. She did not pay anything to get the training but one needed to be a member of the programme and save regularly to get that training.

Bekele (Enani's husband) went to a priest school. She told us that her husband is very good at calculation and record keeping. However, her husband was not at home for us to ask him to show us his documents. *"When he buys one cattle, at the same time he buys the feed. He calculates all the costs incurred to fatten the cattle including medication while he fixes the price to sell"*.

He buys cattle from the market, and a drover (*'neji'*, assigned to bring and/or take cattle from one place to another, usually for long distances) paid 5 birr per cattle, brings them back to his place. The drover brings all the cattle merchants buy from a specific market. The merchants put different marks or signs using different colour paints. Bekele usually uses red paint to identify his cattle. The merchants enter an agreement to make the drover responsible to pay the cost of the cattle, if lost. When Bekele resells the cattle, he has to remove the red mark from the cattle to ensure that the cattle are grown and well fed at home.

When Bekele sells cattle for farming, he signs an agreement for a specific period of time with the buyer to prove that the cattle the customer has bought are healthy. If anything happens within the agreed time period, Bekele will pay back the money.

Enani is an active member of a women's empowerment programme. She keeps the group's cash box at her home. She showed us her saving passbook and cash box with three padlocks. Enani is one of the management committee for her group and serves as a treasurer. Her group has 25 members. As we were told, she was elected by the group members as a treasurer because she can read and write better than the other members. She told us that the programme has brought changes in attitudes among the women, such as the value of saving, women coming together to meet and share social concerns, etc.

Literacy and Numeracy in Livelihoods 85

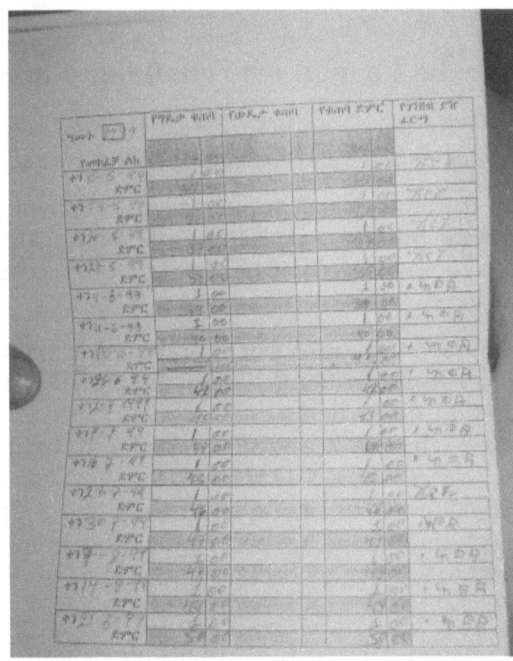

Savings passbook and cash box for group

… Everyday Literacies in Africa

CASE STUDY 8
Literacy and Numeracy in Life Histories

Enani's story raises the issue of literacy and numeracy in the context of life histories. Local literacy and numeracy practices occur outside of livelihoods. The following case studies raise questions about such practices in terms of life histories.

The first two of these case studies (Case Studies 7 and 8) are very short. They are what can be called 'snatch case studies', that is, an opportunity presents itself and is taken even though there is not enough time to undertake a full interview and observation. Both raise more questions than they answer but they provide telling information about the literacy and numeracy practices of some people called by the rest of society 'illiterate'.

Note: all names in these case studies have been changed to prevent identification.

The case of Abebe – a man who challenges life through begging

These two short case studies were prepared by Dr Messeret.

I wanted to map the literacy and numeracy environment with a view to exploring how the findings of the ethnographic research study can feed into the development scenario. In the light of this context I dealt with Abebe's case.

One foggy Sunday morning I went to pray at St. Yared Church, just a few metres away from my home. Following the end of the weekly Sunday Eucharist, I sat down in a tent reserved for the congregation as the rain began to drizzle. A beggar dressed with Dritto [a shabby cloth patched in different places] entered the tent. For a couple of minutes, he walked around begging and finally he sat down next to me. After giving him one birr, as part of my ethnographic study, I began asking him to tell me his background and what does life look like in begging?

After expressing his consent to share his life experience, the man began narrating the story right from his childhood. Accordingly, he introduced himself to be Abebe. He was born at Debre Tabore in the southern part of the province of Gondar. He then went on to tell me that he engaged in farming at his birthplace. Regarding his family, Abebe told me that he had been married to a woman living in his locality and blessed with a daughter. According to him, the marriage didn't last long and it was dissolved through divorce. He added that currently his daughter was living with his parents at Debre Tabore.

When I asked him why he was divorced, he paused, at a loss for words and confessed to me that his sexual dysfunction was the reason for the divorce. With a deep grimace and pathetic voice, he told me that owing to his impotence; his wife could no longer endure living with him. Thereafter, *"I found myself in deep psychological trauma which was aggravated by a disease called Leshimenia which I contracted just a year after the dissolution of the marriage"*, he added. According to his explanation, Leshimenia is a disease characterised by spots of wounds on the skin. This event led him to come to Addis Ababa in search of treatment. As he told me, though he got free treatment for three months in the Black Lion Hospital, he ran out of money during the course of his treatment.

Following this, the hospital ended the treatment and discharged him. Thereafter, he was faced with a serious financial crisis to make ends meet. Since he was unable to engage in any work compatible with his health condition, he made a decision to lead his life as a beggar.

Abebe explained to me that in the early days of his career as a beggar, his daily income reached an average of ten birr. Nonetheless, as time went on, he managed to get more money and much better sums especially during holidays. When he got a relatively large amount of money, Abebe was sending some of this money through merchants to assist his daughter who was a Grade Seven student at Debre Tabor. Abebe lends money for one month only to individuals whom he trusts to the amount of one hundred birr in return for interest at 5%, a rate which would give an annual interest rate of more than 60%. In other cases when he got an amount less than one hundred birr, he would hoard it in pockets he had made in different places in his patched Dritto. In such a way, he succeeded in avoiding the identification of his place of deposit by other persons who could hardly realise that his old patched clothes serve to keep money.

Abebe said that he is illiterate; however, through experience he has learned to count numbers through a repeated act of counting on his fingers. He told me that he is counting in units of 12 up to 3000 birr by using the fingers of both the right and left hands, counting three units to one finger. As a result, Abebe realised that he deposited cash in his pockets amounting to three thousand birr. As time went on, he came up with his own system to remember the whole amount of money he owns through begging. In line with this, he attached buttons to his Dritto, each of which represents a thousand birr – at present three buttons for three thousand birr. Through this mechanism, he managed to know the money he collected through begging.

Abebe assured me that he has no intention of abandoning his begging life as he is getting a good income from it. In addition to this, he told me that he has no plans of returning home although his health is improved, and that it would be difficult to him to get any better job in his home town. Instead, Abebe stressed that he pursues his begging life and collects as much money as he can to improve his life and assist his daughter.

From the foregoing story, we can learn that Abebe has succeeded to overcome the challenges of life by his wisdom and creative thinking despite his illiteracy.

CASE STUDY 9

Almaz: A Story of a Young Illiterate Woman who Won a Court Case

During my semester break on 5 March 2008, I went to the Federal First Instance Court of Addis Ababa (Yeka division) to visit a friend of mine who serves as a judge in the civil Bench of the court. As he was on duty entertaining cases, I decided to wait for him in the courtyard until the court session was adjourned. Accordingly, I took my rest in the enclosed area reserved for visitors and parties having a case in the court. A couple of minutes after my arrival, a young woman came and pulled up a chair and sat down beside me. As time went on, I felt bored waiting for him and decided to talk to the lady who sat next to me. I started my chat by introducing myself and asking her name[4]. Further, I asked her to tell me why she came to the court. Then the woman introduced her name to be Almaz Girma and told me that

---

4   The conversation took place in Amharic

she appeared in the court in order to collect a copy of a court decision from the registrar (the verdict was written in Amharic).

While waiting, I asked her if she would be willing to tell me the subject matter of the case. She expressed her consent to talk about the case by nodding her head. Almaz explained to me that the case decided by the court pertains to an application she made in this court of law some six months back requesting a court order pronouncing the existence of paternal filiations between her child and her deceased partner. Furthermore, she noted that the relief sought in the application also included a declaration that her child is entitled to a share of the inheritance left by the deceased. At this juncture, I requested Almaz to elaborate as to how she came across the man she claimed to have had a love affair with and the reason for bringing a legal action. The woman then went on to narrate the whole story from the moment she began her romantic relationship till it ended and led her to apply for the court order.

Almaz began her story starting from the reason why she came to Addis. According to her, she came to the city to seek work. Almaz told me that upon her arrival, she went to her relatives who were residing in Bole area and stayed there for a short period of time. During her stay, she requested them to help her to get a job with a reasonable wage which would assist her to make her living. Nonetheless, *"their knowledge concerning my illiterate background prompted them to advise me that I had better look for low-profile jobs"*, she said. She then told me that her relatives helped her to become employed as a housemaid in the home of a well-to-do family residing in their locality.

As she told me, it was at this moment that the romantic relationship with her deceased partner began. At that time, the head of the family named Bulla approached Almaz to have sexual intercourse secretly. In due course, Bulla made repeated attempts to persuade her to engage in sexual intercourse, knowing her status in the house; she refused to accept the request but. One day, in his wife's and his children's absence, Bulla forced her to have sexual intercourse. Subsequently, Almaz confessed to me that they continued to have repeated sexual intercourse.

On one occasion, Bulla's wife caught them red-handed making love in her bed. The next day, the indignant wife Melat expelled Almaz from her home. Following this, Almaz began to live in a private residential flat independently and because of their prejudice, she was not in a position to inform her relatives of her unhappy situation. In contrast to Melat's expectation that the situation would break Almaz's tie with Bulla, however, the two continued their romantic affair in secret. According to Almaz, Bulla increased in his affection towards her to the extent of covering her livelihood. A few months after her relocation into the new flat, she gave birth to a baby boy. When she disclosed this fact to Bulla, he congratulated her for bearing the child and promised her that he would do his level best to raise the child and told her that the baby was his son.

Thereafter, Bulla made frequent appearances at her home and extended necessary assistance for her and the child. Apart from the financial support he made to the child, Bulla manifested his paternity towards the child by taking such measures as signing documents revealing the child's identity. Unfortunately, Almaz told me that Bulla died in a car accident.

At this point, I asked her what measures did she take after this incident. Almaz said that she did not take any concrete step until the time her cousin came to visit her. One bright morning, "my cousin who was studying at the Addis Ababa University came to visit me. I then told him the whole story what happened to me and asked him to give me some advice on what to do", she responded. "He then offered me advice to bring a legal action before a court of law seeking for a pronouncement of fatherhood". Then Almaz outlined the events in the following words.

"Replying to my request for advice, my cousin after consulting a resource person proposed to me that I should institute a legal action demanding a court order confirming that the newly born child is the son of Bulla. Besides this, he emphasised to me the need for making an additional claim seeking for a decision entitling my son to a share in the inheritance from Bulla's property. I accepted his advice but told him that the cost of preparing the application and the court fee were not affordable to me. Fortunately, he understood my financial condition and he covered the cost required to prepare the application. As to the court fee, he helped me to get a certificate from the local kebel (town administrative organ) revealing my poor financial status, which would help me to apply in the court of law without the need to pay a court fee.

After the completion of these important steps, I made an application to the court to substantiate my claim. I presented the following evidences":

1. Oral witnesses who testified that Bulla treated the child as his son.
2. A birth certificate on which Bulla had put his signature in the space provided for parents.
3. Several private letters he communicated to me citing his concern for the health of the child and stressing that the child is his beloved son

Then I asked her where and how, despite her illiteracy, she had gained an understanding of recording these three evidences. She said, "I know that my life is very much in danger and I am not able to make my living and to raise my beloved child in my poor situation. Thus I am well aware of the situation. I also learned many things in the house I was working with, particularly when relatives were chatting during festivals. This gave me an opportunity to realise the importance of keeping these evidences to substantiate my claim. To my surprise, the said evidences were proved to be sound to back my argument, and the court passed a verdict in favour of me."

She said that the order in the court's verdict contained the following:

The value of Bulla's family capital worth 1,500,000 birr be apportioned to his wife Melat on the one hand and his three children, two from Melat and the one he got from Almaz

A sum of 750,000 birr is reserved for Melat as her share of the communal property and the remaining 750,000 is to be equally divided between the three children.

The share of her child to the amount of 250,000 birr is given to Almaz as the mother and tutor of the former.

I found the case to be educative in that, despite her illiteracy, the woman was able to understand the fact that the evidences she brought to the court are relevant to her claim. Moreover, this case study built up a picture of how some people progress in literacy and increase in the community to which they belong.

CASE STUDY 10
Literacy and Numeracy in Rural Lives

Literacy and numeracy practices do not just occur in urban areas and markets – as the story of Enani shows. The following case studies come from rural areas – women and men farmers and their families.

The case of Ayelech: An artist in mud

Compiled by Negussie Hailu, Agri Service Ethiopia

This case study is conducted in Enebse Sar Mider *woreda* which is located in the northwestern part of Ethiopia, Amhara National Regional State. The subject of the case study is living in one of the kebele located nine km from Mertule Mariam town (an ancient town that serves as the capital of the *woreda*). I made the field visit on the 3rd of January 2008 to collect the data necessary for compiling the case study. The methods I used to collect the data were village walk and observation, informal/ unstructured interview, and photographs.

I went to the area at first to collect additional data for the case study I started earlier on Edir, a social organisation established by the community mainly to facilitate a funeral ceremony. At the time of my arrival, the people whom I should have contacted arrived late at the appointed place. Until they came, I wandered around and saw three people threshing grain on the ground using cows and oxen. After greeting, as usual, I asked them about their harvest. I explained my wish to visit their home if they would agree and if it was not far away. They told me that they would be very glad to show me if I waited for some time until somebody would come and take the work on the threshing (one of them told me that he was waiting for his son to come there to help them and promised to accompany me on his arrival).

Farmers threshing grain on the ground

At that moment, I saw two women coming in our direction carrying water pots on their back. One of them went apart in another direction, while the other one came nearer to pass to her home on the nearby road. Before passing, she greeted us (it is not uncommon to greet or to be greeted by everybody, whether he/she is a stranger or not), and continued her journey. Suddenly, I asked her permission to allow me to take her photo. She smiled and stopped, shrugging her shoulders in a manner that explained her acceptance of my request. I took enough pictures and then I raised another question; "May I visit your home, please?" I asked. When the men heard my request, they told me that her home was nearer and insisted that I go with her. Still, I asked one of them to accompany me since I was afraid to go with her alone. I felt that I must be cautious not to violate the norms of that community (entering someone's home particularly in the absence of the head of the house, the husband, might create a bad feeling, and may even be result in conflict to the extent of losing one's life). They understood my worry and assured me that there wouldn't be any danger. I followed her to her home and arrived near the compound.

Zenebu carrying a pot filled with water

On the way I asked her about her family and what her name was. She said she was Zenebu Adamu, 22, and married with one child.

Unlike the settlement of other rural villages, the one I visited was dense and seemed well planned. The houses are constructed in rows. When we entered the village, I stopped outside the compound of her home until invited to enter. She invited me and I entered the compound. I found the compound very clean and well organised. Before I went into the house, I looked intently at all the corners of the compound. I couldn't believe my eyes, it was beyond my expectation. The roof of the house was made of corrugated iron sheet and the wall was well plastered with mud and cow/ox dung. There were two rooms sharing the same roof. There were other small rooms constructed with simple materials but not plastered as the bigger one. I whispered to myself, 'Is it really a farmer's house?'

What caught my eye were the drawings and texts written on the wall. First, I couldn't realise the drawings and fixed my eyes on the texts and read them carefully. Two texts were written in Amharic – the local as well as the national language - and contained a sort of proverb/slogan and poems.

Wall writings: The texts are translated in the following way:

1. I know that a friend of today is tomorrow's enemy, Knowing this, I prefer to be alone to extend my existence.
2. Take off your gossip bonnet before you come into this house!

Here again, I had to stop outside until I was invited to enter the house. Zenebu entered one of the rooms and came back after putting down the water pot. Standing at the door with her little daughter, she invited me to enter the house.

When the sheep heard her sound, they came in from the outside and pointing their heads towards her expecting to get something (it seemed they were begging her to drop something into their mouth).

Zenebu feeding the sheep

Instead of accepting her invitation, I moved closer to the wall to look at the pictures. I was extremely excited to be there and very surprised with the events which had happened without my intention. Since I was not satisfied with the data I collected from the other village, I was very eager to explore all that had happened here. And I assumed that the place was the right place for and the home of ethnography. Indeed, attracted by the events, I had forgotten the appointment I had outside and decided to stay there.

Literacy and Numeracy in Livelihoods 97

Zenebu gave some feed to the sheep and came to me, still begging me to enter her home. Meanwhile, a lady came out of another room and saw me with surprise; she greeted me with some reservation because she didn't expect a man to have appeared there in her compound. I replied respectfully. I told her my name and address. She became glad and smiled when I told her from which organisation I am. And I tried to hide my excitement and started to raise some other social and economic issues that led me to the major agenda. In addition, Zenebu tried to introduce me to the lady and told me that she was her mother-in-law.

Ayelech standing in front of the gate

Her name is Ayelech. *"All these drawings are Ayelech's product of her long experience in life"*, said Zenebu. She also told me that her home management was unique in the area. All what I heard from Zenebu increased my eagerness to know more about the lady Ayelech and the events there.

Ayelech Yibeltal is 48, widowed and has 5 children (2 female); two of them (1 male and 1 female) are married and the other three (two male and 1 female) are living with her although two of them are attending their education (grade12 and 10) at Mertule Mariam and come home every Saturday. Her elder son (Zenebu's husband) is living in the next room and is responsible to support her in the preparation of her farm plot otherwise she is living independently. After her husband died, she took all the responsibilities and manages everything by herself. I changed my mind and decided to enter Ayelech's room instead of Zenebu's. But I decided to stay for some time outside raising questions about the texts and drawings on the wall.

I asked Ayelech whose drawings these were and why they had been drawn. [The drawings are not painted with brushes. Nor are they sketched with pencils. Rather they are made from mud. They are a sort of moulds/sculptures. She used charcoal, ash or limestone to paint hair and other parts of the drawings].

She started telling me the story. "All the drawings are mine. The texts are written by my daughter. I can't read and write. I have had a good friendship with mud throughout my life. You can do everything with mud. I drew these pictures long ago [pointing to the pictures by her chin]. They represent members of the family. Look, they are five in number. Remember I told you that I have five children."

Ayelech's drawings representing her children

Ayelech's drawings

'These five pictures represent my five children; of course they are not exactly their pictures. It is only to represent. I drafted these pictures (pointing to the other one) recently when my son got married with Zenebu. I have the oldest pictures at the back wall." She paused to check whether I am interested to see them or not. I showed my interest and we moved together to the back side of the house.

We had to cross the 'family room' to go out through the back gate. She showed me the pictures. "These [pointing her finger to the picture] represented my husband and me."

Ayelech's drawings representing her husband and herself

Note the cross in the middle

"I have a strong belief in a one-to-one marriage. For this, our religion (Christianity) is the base. That is why I put the cross in between our pictures. I believe this teaches others also. We (with her husband) passed many ups and downs together. He appreciated all my works. All our materials we are using - the bed, shelves, box, chair, table, grain store, etc are made of mud. I have no time to waste. I am always busy in making something from mud. That is why I said I have a good friendship with mud". From her explanations and voice, one can easily observe her inner emotions and compassions.

There was also another picture which represents mother and child.

Ayelech's drawing representing mother and child

I took out a picture from my pocket and asked her whether she knows the picture or not. She smiled and told me that the picture is St. Mary and The Son. Then I asked, "How do you know?" "I know this picture since my childhood. As an Orthodox Christian, I usually go to church and I saw it there and you can find this picture everywhere among the community. And you can find this picture in the books prepared for prayer." I raised another question: "Do you have any such books at home?" "No, I do not have. Since I am illiterate [Mehayim in Amharic] I do not have it. But my children have lots of such books. Usually they read for me and I enjoy hearing it and looking at the pictures in it." I did this because I saw in her drawing a picture similar to this one. Putting the one which I had behind the drawing, I asked, "Does this represent the same?" She laughed and said, "No, that was not my intention. I sketched it to express mother's love to her child. Since my drawings are not as perfect as other pictures, it is immoral for me to compare the Lady and The Son with this one". And she took the picture from my hand and kissed it and she did not want to continue the discussion any more. Instead she led me to the other works.

To show me what she was making, she turned her face to the back, moving forward and said: "Look at that storage. That is what I am making now. It is for grain/flour storage. Most of us here in the locality using such a storage". The storage she was making was purely made from mud. It has layers.

A mud-made storage with layers mostly for grains

A mud-made storage mostly for flour

Look at the layers, I asked the lady to tell me the purpose of the layers. She told me that the layers have three functions. *"1. It makes the construction very easy and strong. 2. You can easily take out the grain/flour by pulling out the layers turn by turn. 3. You can measure/estimate the amount of grain you have left in it."* She said that it is estimated that one layer contains one *'Dirib'* – a local unit of measurement that contains twelve 'Sahin' – again another unit of measurement (it is a dish) which all the people in this area use in selling and buying grains. 'Sahin' is a factory-made material available in the market. But Ayelech has her own material made of mud that exactly measures the same amount of grain where a 'Sahin' measures. We measured it while we sat and discussed other issues. As she said, one 'Dirib' is equal to twelve 'Sahin'. And I measured the aforementioned amounts in kilogrammes after I came back home. The twelve 'Sahin' grain measured almost equal to seventeen kilogrammes.

'Sahin' **a measurement material**

She requested me to accept her apologies for making me stay outside without requesting me to enter her home for coffee and something to eat and she forced me to enter. I accepted her invitation and entered the house following her. As I said, unlike other rural homes (I know many of the rural houses are not so clean and well organised), hers is clean and well decorated. Moreover, the utensils are kept properly on the shelves made from mud by her wisdom.

The shelves constructed on the wall for utensils: Look at the drawings decorations

As one can see from the pictures, all the cups, glasses, bottles, pots, and others have their own place. I raised a question that came into my mind. "Why do you do all this?" "You know", she replied, "You can easily pick a tool which you want without any problem. The other thing is that you can keep it always clean and anybody who wants to use it, whether he is a family member or guest - during mourning for example, can get it easily without waiting for the owner". "Most importantly", she continued, "you can extend its years of service. As you see, it is not accessible to children".

During my observation, I saw relatively bigger shelf-like materials planted on the two opposite sides of the wall. These shelves were also made from mud. The one which was behind me had a window and a mosquito net was stretched covering the window opening. The one which was in front of me had a rawhide on it. When I saw the leather, I realised that these two shelves were beds, because I know and I myself have had the experience that in many rural parts of Ethiopia, the rawhide serves as a mattress.

Literacy and Numeracy in Livelihoods 105

An overlapping bed: Look at the layers

A bed with mosquito net

The shelves have three layers. The lower one serves to keep shoes and other materials. The second and the third serve as beds; the second one is for babies as it is nearer to the floor and the third for adults. I asked Ayelech why she stretched the mosquito net on the opening of the bed. *"It is provided by the health agents and it serves to protect from mosquito bites. It is very useful"*. I extended my question, "But the net is not properly hung. It allows mosquitoes to enter to the bed. Is it in this way that...?" She immediately interrupted me before I finished my question and said, *"No, no, it is not in this way that I was trained. It must be hung properly in that it couldn't allow mosquitoes to enter. You see these beds are far better than the one made from wood and a rope that you stretched on the floor. The two or three sides of my beds are walls I only need to protect the mosquitoes from one or two sides. Mine is much better to control them. Look, this one is hung to cover the two sides. Yes, as you said, this is not stretched properly. This season is not that much dangerous. At other times, I stretch it very tightly. I know the benefit of this net very well"*.

She started to make coffee. But I refused the coffee and accept her request only to eat my lunch. I know what would happen if I refused all the invitations. She cooked a sauce (called *Shiro Wot* in Amharic) very quickly. She didn't use any flat wooden material to chop the onions. She simply used a knife and her hand. She served me a very nice lunch. The sauce was my favourite and cooked in a way that goes well with my health. It was really very tasty and I questioned her about her upbringing in the rural area and asked whether she stayed in the towns or not. But she told me that she did not know even the Woreda (District) town – Mertule Mariam very well. She never ever goes to the towns or cities other than this town. Even she goes to this town only on marketdays for marketing.

Literacy and Numeracy in Livelihoods 107

Cooking

After lunch, I raised the following question: "Have you paid the land tax regularly?" Her answer was fast and positive. She told me that she had already paid the previous year's tax and she is going to pay this year's pretty soon after she collects her grains from the field. "What other payment should you settle? How do you collect the receipts and where do you put them?" These were the next questions I asked.

108   *Everyday Literacies in Africa*

Ayelech identifying the receipts: look at her fingers

In answering the question, she tried to show me her caution. She collected the receipts from the concerned body who requested her for payments. The farm land taxes, the church membership fee, payments for Red Cross Society, and Sport are some of her compulsory payments. She put all the receipts in her box, which is mainly made to keep clothes of the family. On my request, she brought some of the receipts from the box (she did not volunteer to show me the box). When I asked her to give me first the receipt of the land tax, she selected from among the others quickly and gave me. I read the receipt and it was exactly the receipt collected for the payment of farming land tax. *"This is the church receipt and this one is the Red Cross,"* she presented them turn by turn and asked me whether she selected correctly or not. I confirmed that she had done it correctly. She was not sure only about one of the receipts she brought. I took the receipt from her hand and told her to read the title of the receipt like the others, to see whether she identified the others by reading. But she replied in this way: *"Do not be mistaken. I couldn't read and write"*. I asked, "If so how do you identify the receipts?" She took the receipts and started her answer for the question in the following way:

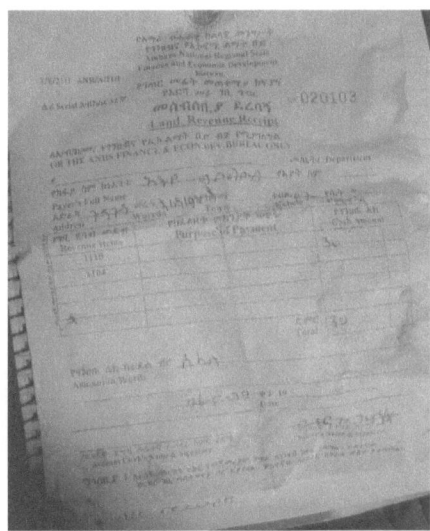

A receipt for farm land rent/tax

She picked out the receipt for the land tax and told me, "Look, this one is larger in size than the others and the receipts I collected for such purpose are very thin, and relatively soft. Look at the others they are small in size and a little bit thick and rough. I can identify some of them using the emblems attached with the receipts (church and Red Cross)." Finally she concluded, "It is in this way that I usually identify the receipts."

Receipts identified by their emblems

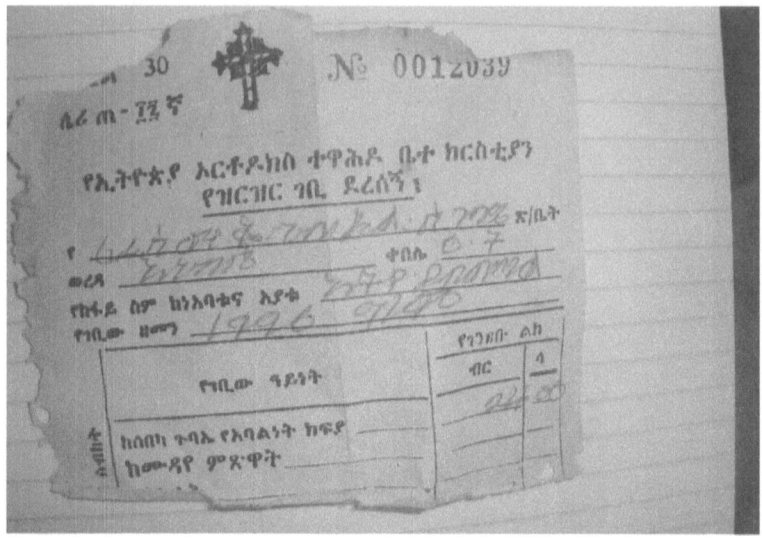

Receipts identified by their emblems

During our discussion and my stay with her, I had the opportunity to observe Ayelech's hands. They are very rough and deformed. I felt bad when I looked at her hands. I think they took the current shape due to her unreserved and devoted work on mud to produce many things and her work on the farmland.

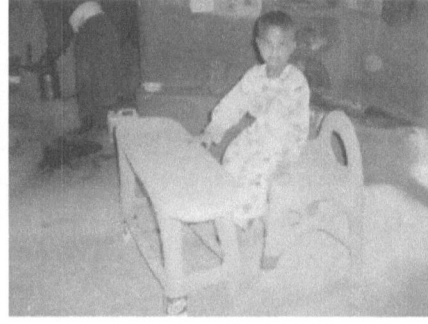

Some of the house furniture

Ayelech and her mud working

Finally I raised the following question: "You told me that you can't read and write. As you may remember, there was a literacy campaign in the 1970's all over the country. I know that many adults were able to read and write as a result of that campaign. Didn't you participate in that programme?" "I did", she replied with regret, "But we were not that much conscious and interested to attend the classes. Do you know what I did? I took some eggs [as a bribe] to the teacher and he filled in the attendance sheet as if I was present. Since I didn't attend the programme, properly today I remain illiterate. I can identify some of the letters but with many problems". But with all her skills and knowledge, should we label Ayelech as illiterate?

Another time, when I travelled to a village next to Ayelech's village, I stopped there for a while and made a visit to that particular area and checked the houses of her neighbours. I visited two houses and observed that they are managing their home in a similar way except the drawings. I asked them how they develop such a skill. Unanimously, they told me that it was mainly the influence of Ayelech; they learned from her.

These are some of the points that I find out from this case study. But, there are still so many other literacy events in the house of this lady which include pictures pasted on the inside wall, texts written on the wall, printed texts (like newspapers) pasted on the wall, etc. The writer of this paper leaves these things untouched due to time shortage. All these will have their own contribution to the intended purpose. So I strongly recommend further exploration and preparation of additional case studies on the same subject.

CASE STUDY 11
A Farming Family

This case study was conducted by a team of two staff of ADA, Girma Yeshanew and Solomon Tadesse.

This paper reports on a case study which focuses on literacy and numeracy practices of farmers, both men and women, of Ambomesk locality in Mecha *woreda*, west Gojam zone, Amhara Region. Specifically the case study involves a husband and wife, Ato Genet and W/ro Mulu, who are residing in that locality and participating in the Functional Adult Literacy (FAL) Programme implemented by Amhara Development Association (ADA) in collaboration with IIZ/DVV.

Information was gathered using ethnographic research perspective including interview, observation and discussion. The findings of the case study have two important dimensions. On the one hand there are literacy related practices within the household as a result of literacy programmes and supports given by different actors including ADA. On the other hand and more important was the finding that people also have their own indigenous and tradition-based skills and knowledge of numeracy and literacy practices applied in the day to day life.

It was on Monday 10 February 2008 that we travelled to Ambomesk to meet two participants in the ADA-FAL programme, Ato Genet and W/ro Mulu at the kebele office, which is a mile away from their home. While we were going back to their home, we had the opportunity to talk about issues related to their life. That helped us easily to start discussion and build trust.

As we went into their house, we were invited to sit on the *medeb*, a traditional seat made of stone and mud. As we prepared ourselves to start the discussion with Genet and Mulu, the team had the opportunity to observe the insides of their small *tukul*. Like most rural houses, that small *tukul* was subdivided into three small parts, where one part is for keeping the cattle, the second serving as '*gotera*' for keeping grain, and the third for bedroom and living room. We also saw in one corner a shelf made of mud for keeping the household utensils.

Just as an ice breaker, we started the discussion with what we had seen in that small *tukul*. We asked them, "Why are the animals living together with you in the same room?" W/ro Mulu said, *"It is for security that we live together. If we don't watch our cattle properly, a thief would come and raid them out."* Her response was interesting in that we learned that it is a tradition to live with their cattle; they highly value them and consider them to be a member of the household. Although the cattle are living with them, we observed that the house is not as messy as one would expect. Mulu and Genet seem to be quite vigilant in maintaining cleanliness and order in their room. Considering this as one important issue related to our subject, we asked Mulu another question. "Your house is so clean and orderly, can you tell us how and why you do that?" She responded by relating to the health education and advice given by health extension workers in the village. She said, "The health extension worker, Zenebech, has taught us how to keep our house clean and where to dispose of garbage and dirt. She also taught us that we get ill if we don't keep ourselves clean."

The team was aware that Mulu was one of the beneficiaries of the credit scheme linked with the FAL programme. We asked her what she had done with the money she borrowed from the FAL programme. She told us that she had taken 1000 birr credit and added 500 birr from own saving and bought an ox. She did the fattening for four months and sold it for more than 1800 birr, and she obtained a profit 300 birr out of it. We asked her, "What about the forage the ox consumed in the fattening. Didn't it cost you?" She replied, *"We didn't buy any; there was only grazing in the field and feeding hay we had for our other ox and cow."*

During our discussion, we came to know that the main source of income of the couple is agriculture. They have two 'kada', equivalent to a half hectare, land for growing millet and 'daggusa', a grass type cereal with very small grain. They cultivate the land only once in a year. They produce only 400 kg of daggusa and 900 kg of millet in one harvesting season, and they affirmed that it cannot satisfy their needs to feed themselves until the next harvest season. Mulu said, "To overcome this problem both of us were engaged in other income generating activities on top of the farming. My husband works as a daily labourer in the town and I prepare arakie, the local spirit, to sell in the market." She continued narrating her story how she started preparing arakie. "Unlike many other newly married couples, we had nobody to give us any presents as is accustomed in our culture. I lost both my parents when I was a child. I grew up with my sister. Then I moved to the town, Merawi, to work as a housemaid. That is when I met Genetu, my husband, who had been working as a guard in our neighbour's house.

When the government was conducting the land redistribution programme, my uncle helped me secure my parents' land. Having land to farm, I was forced to go back to the village and settle there. This made me and Genetu think about marriage. He brought one ox and we started to live together as husband and wife. We just started our marriage with out a 'gabi', (a local shawl made of cotton) to wear when we sleep. We were feeling cold at night. I was wondering what to do to buy night clothes or a blanket. A thought had come to my mind, preparing arakie to sell. However, I had no experience on how to prepare it, I didn't have a mother to show me how to prepare it either. While I was thinking, an idea came to my mind, consulting my aunt. I know she prepares arakie for holidays. Immediately I went to Merawi where my aunt is living. When I raised the issue of her preparing arakie for selling in the market, at first she was hesitant, afraid of going to the open market. Finally, she agreed to prepare the spirit and let me sell it in the market. We partnered for some time, working together and sharing the profit. In the meantime, I started learning how to prepare arakie. Consequently, I started to prepare the arakie all by myself. Since then I have been preparing arakie and sell it to the wholesaler."

We asked her, 'How do you calculate the profit and keep a record?' She told us that since she had lost her parents at an early stage in her life, she had never joined the formal school but she can calculate the balance and keep everything in her mind. She started telling us how she calculates the profit. "I use 5 kilo daggusa for 14 birr, 25 kilo of millet for 55 birr , 10 big cups of germinated barley for 25 birr, and 2 kilo of gesho for 8 birr. I obtain 17 litres of arakie out of it. It costs 2.70 birr for grinding the grains. I will invest a total of 112.70 birr to get 17 litres of arakie. I will sell a litre of arakie for 8.5 birr, which will bring me 144.5 birr. I get 31birr profit." The process for making arakie takes 10 solid days. We realised that the wood that is used as a fuel for distillation and the labour she expended are not considered as expense to calculate the actual profit. We were very surprised by her quick and perfect calculation skills. We asked her to show us how she adds and subtracts numbers without writing them. She replied that "When the numbers are big, I use sticks and count; otherwise I do them in my heart."

Immediately Genetu brought sticks from the garden and broke them into equal pieces. Then he started to show us how his wife uses sticks to calculate. He gave us an example. "If I want to add, for example, 67 and 36, first, I put 6 sticks to the left, then add 3 sticks which each sticks represents tens. I then put 7 sticks to the right and added 6 sticks where each stick represents ones. The six and three sticks placed at the left together made 9 sticks which is 90 and the sticks from the left side count up to be 13, which is ten and three, therefore the total will be 103."

Literacy and Numeracy in Livelihoods 115

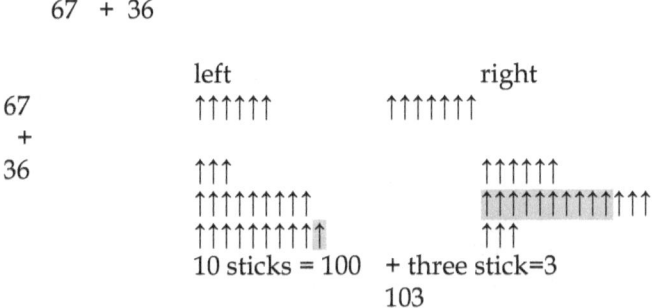

Remembering the discussion we had while travelling in the car about the lesson she took in the FAL centre on poultry, we asked her, 'Why do you prefer this activity than other income-generating activities like poultry?" She said, "The other activity we were engaged in was poultry some time ago. But an epidemic erupted, killing a large number of hens in the village. We sold our chickens at low prices so as not to be a victim of the epidemic. Though we were taught on modern poultry and the vaccination for disease prevention, we found it very laborious and costly. Moreover, fodder for the chicken is not easily available. It requires investing huge money compared to arakie preparation. Distillation and selling arakie is relatively simple and less costly". She added, "Poultry need additional manpower that stays around when we are away from the house." We asked her, "Do you think that having a child is a solution to solve the problem?" She said, "No, it is not a solution, rather a burden. We have to have enough wealth to do so. Therefore, I am taking a contraceptive not to have a child. Sometime in the future we have a plan to have one or two children."

Ato Genet, her husband, is fighting poverty by engaging himself in different activities. He is working as a daily labourer obtaining 15 to 20 birr per day besides farming. He told us he and all participants in the FAL centre took practical lessons on nursery growing, which helped them to cultivate and sell plants for people who want to plant in their land. Now he is preparing seedlings of eucalyptus trees and green pepper to sell in the coming summer.

While we were observing the house, searching for any written documents, we saw a paper wrapped with plastic and hanging on the wall. We asked the husband what it says and why it is kept carefully.

He said, "We built a toilet and use it properly; that is important to prevent contaminated diseases. We constructed a fuel-saving stove, a mud shelf for household utensils, and a ground well for dry waste disposal. Because of these and the like activities, we were selected as a model farmer and awarded a certificate by the woreda health office."

Finally, we asked them, "Why do you need literacy?". They said, "We need literacy to keep and maintain our detailed records, to read and count numbers, not to be cheated by some merchants and to keep our health well." But there are no signs that in fact they keep such records, and it is clear from their counting systems that they do not use paper to calculate their accounts. The FAL programme was more useful to them for its social improvements than for the written forms of literacy and numeracy taught.

We noticed that the couple are fighting poverty as much as they can. They have their own forms of literacy and numeracy skills that help their daily activities. What kind of literacy centre will help them develop the type of literacy they need?

PART II

Some Findings from the Case Studies and their Implications for Teaching Literacy and Numeracy to Adults

3

Teaching Literacy and Numeracy to Adults

Many ethnographic studies of local literacy and numeracy practices have been conducted and published in many parts of the world (Street 1995, 2001; Prinsloo and Breier 1997; Mahiri 2004 etc). But such surveys often lead to the doubting question, 'So what?' What is the value of such accounts? What is their relevance to our literacy learning programmes? How can they be of practical use to those who plan learning programmes and those who teach in them? This part of the book seeks to address these questions.

This section is based mainly on the work undertaken in the third LETTER ETHIOPIA workshop in April-May 2008 in Debre Zeit, Ethiopia, but it also draws on the whole programme. It falls into two main parts:

(i) Some general conclusions from our field work, some of the lessons we are able to draw out from the case studies

(ii) An analysis of some of the implications of those lessons for our adult literacy learning programmes

Some conclusions

The lessons which we have chosen to describe here fall into two parts – those concerning literacy and numeracy, and a number of other findings which struck us as being relevant to our theme.

Literacy and numeracy findings

The workshop participants welcomed some visitors from the Government of Ethiopia and from donor and development agencies on the last full day of the workshop. In preparation for that, a number of key points arising from the LETTER programme were prepared and presented to the visitors (they appear below in the boxes). What follows is an expanded version of these key points.

1. We were struck by the fact that people we labelled as 'illiterates' are engaged in literacy and numeracy activities **in their daily social practices.** Many of our informants who call themselves 'illiterate' nevertheless engaged in literacy practices. Ade told us that she cannot read and write, but she can count. Mulu said that since she had lost her parents at an early stage in her life, she had never joined the formal school but she can calculate the balance and keep everything in her mind. Almaz said of her relations in Addis Ababa, *"their knowledge concerning my illiterate background prompted them to advise me that I had better look for low-profile jobs"*. All these use literacy texts in various ways. Almaz could not have progressed with her law suit without access to and using the many documents in the case including letters sent to her and birth certificates. Genet the farmer valued the certificate he had received and hung it on his walls, although he too said he was 'illiterate'. Ayelech put it clearly: When asked whether she had in her home any books similar to the ones she had described, she replied: *"No, I do not have. Since I am illiterate [Mehayim in Amharic] I do not have them. But my children have lots of such books. Usually they read for me and I enjoy hearing it and looking at the pictures in it."*

So these so-called 'illiterates' negotiate the literate world. Some of this of course they manage by mediation. *"Our children in school write the loan and the income on separate sheets of paper."* Ayelech got her daughter to write her proverbs and poems on the walls of her houses. The women who shared their small-scale shopkeeping in Tigray also shared their literacy skills. Efe used the village priest to consult her birth records and Enani's husband Bekele kept accounts for her. But equally they sometimes manage by themselves – Ayelech can pick out for herself the different documents she had by their size, their texture and various symbols on them. Almaz can identify the documents she needs by their size and feel.

And they do not feel any great need for learning literacy skills for themselves. If they attend adult literacy learning programmes, it is more for the skills training they can get from them than for learning literacy. As Genet said, he and all participants in the FAL centre took practical lessons on nursery growing, which helped them to cultivate and sell plants for people who want to plant in their land. The literacy element was of less use to them.

And some of our case studies show that people who do have literacy skills often do not use them. The photograph of the small-scale shop shows no signs or labels at all and most of our informants kept their business accounts in their heads rather than on paper. But others do use formal literacy and numeracy skills and benefit from them. Enani became the treasurer of her women's credit and savings group because, as she said, *"she was elected by the group members as a treasurer because she can read and write better than the other members"*.

Such findings challenge many of the assumptions on which our adult literacy learning programmes are based.

2. Our field work, both during the workshops and in our major case studies conducted between the three workshops, revealed that there are multiple literacy and numeracy practices.

> *"We have learned that there are multiple literacies in the homes, the community, the market, workplace, the church and the mosque."*

This is not just a matter of different languages and different scripts, although these do of course exist. Even within one language and one script, there are different literacy practices, different ways of writing and meaning making

We noticed, for example, religious literacy practices – reading the Bible in Geez, for example, or reading the Qu'ran. We noticed shop signs, street notices, and advertisements. We saw writing on the walls of houses and other buildings. We saw the different literacy and numeracy practices associated with different livelihood activities; occupational and commercial literacies. Income generation activities led some people to use their own ways of recording the results of their hard work. We came across examples of bureaucratic literacy, public notices and posters, bills and invoices, and government literacies associated with issues of health, elections and the census. We saw an example of legal literacy. We noted a good deal of social literacy practices, such as informal notes passed among members of a family or friends and text messaging by cellphones is increasing, even among people officially designated as 'illiterate'. We noticed some home or domestic literacy practices: *"While we were observing the house, searching for any written documents, we saw a paper wrapped with plastic and hanging* on the wall. We asked the husband what it says and why it is kept carefully". One example of farming literacy can be seen in the case of Bekele:

> "The merchants put different marks or signs [on their cattle] using different colour paints. Bekele usually uses red paint to identify his cattle. The merchants enter an agreement to make the drover responsible to pay the cost of the cattle, if lost. When Bekele resells the cattle, he has to remove the red mark from the cattle to ensure that the cattle are grown and well fed at home.
>
> When Bekele sells cattle for farming, he signs an agreement for a specific period of time with the buyer to prove that the cattle the customer has bought are healthy. If anything happens within the agreed time period, Bekele will pay back the money."

So we saw many different kinds of literacy practices, unlike the literacy taught in the classroom. We agreed that we can call these 'local' literacy practices.

In particular, we noticed that there are many different kinds of numeracy practices in the home, the market and the street. Local ways of measuring volume, weights and distances are matched by individual ways of counting (using buttons, sticks or beans/grains/seeds). Some of these ways of measuring were individual but many were communal, used by all who operated in that market. There is among the people we are trying to teach no one right way to count, measure and calculate.

3. We noticed a number of features of these everyday literacy and numeracy practices.

First, that they were often written using *more than one language and indeed more than one script*. Messages were on several occasions repeated in Amharic, in Afaan Oromo, and in English, using different scripts. And written messages, like so much speech, often combined words from Amharic or another language with words from English, to make a hybrid language. Local people, 'literate' and 'illiterate' negotiated their way through this linguistic jungle almost without recognising what they are doing; they switched from one script to another, from one language to another, without being conscious of it.

Secondly, many of these literacies were *multi-modal* – that is, they combined signs, symbols and pictures together with text. Road signs often had words and symbols on them; advertisements almost always had some picture. Text messages on mobile phones often included some symbol like an emoticon – it is a natural thing to do to send a picture.

Thirdly, we noticed strongly that *numeracy in real life is always integrated with literacy*. There is no such thing in real life as 'three', only 'three somethings' (three cups, children, coats, or cauliflowers etc).

4. We noticed that the local literacy and numeracy practices are often different from those being taught in the adult literacy learning programmes. The last point about the numeracy practices illustrates this. In the taught class, numeracy (in the form of 'sums') are kept separate from writing; in the local numeracy practices, written calculations always have some indication of what the figures mean (money, goods, people, etc).

> We have learned that the literacy and numeracy practices in the homes/community/workplace/churches, mosques are DIFFERENT from the literacy and numeracy practices taught in the classroom

One major difference however is that the literacy practices of the classroom possess a measure of what may be called 'formality', in that they teach us there is a 'right' way to do something and all other ways are 'wrong'. This is shown by the use of a (usually red) tick or cross, itself an interesting academic literacy practice. But the local practices are informal; there are many different ways of spelling words (for example, in a shopping list or in a letter to a family member); there is no one right way to send a 'txt mssg'. Instead there are many different right ways for different people.

The numeracy practices of the classroom teach us there is one right way to add up figures like 27+38 and one right answer, 65. But in real life, what appear at first sight to be simple sums do not have only one answer or at least do not have the formal school answer, as the reports of the workshops show clearly. " 2+2 = 4 is not always true. If you push the elevator button, "2" twice, this will not take you to the 4th floors. If you merge 2 groups of training participants with another 2 groups, you end up with 1 group, not 4."

Ethnographic research into street numeracies has discovered that people use a number of different strategies to calculate. Our case studies show people using maize grains or sticks or other ways of calculating. We also noticed how much calculation is done by estimation rather than by calculation; exactness is not always required in real life. The life of the classroom is an artificial context designed for the purpose of learning certain practices with a preciseness not known in much of daily life.

5. We learned that these different sets of literacy practices have a powerdimension to them. Different values are attached to different sets of literacy and numeracy practices – some are felt to be more valuable than others. The literacy practices of the classroom are regarded as 'the (one and only) literacy', as are the numeracy practices. The other literacies and numeracies are regarded as either not existing at all, or being in some way inferior – they are sometimes called vernacular or even proto-literacies.

We found that even those using these informal local literacies often did not regard them as 'literacy'. Men and women who are writing and reading in their own fashion continue to call themselves 'illiterate' simply because they had not been to school and were able to engage in the formal literacy practices of reading a discursive text and writing without spelling mistakes. The local literacies 'did not count' as literacy to them and to many others. Rather than seeing these as different but equal forms of literacy and numeracy, society in general elevated the formal schooled literacy above all other forms of literacy. The schooled literacy carries with it status in society, the informal literacies do not have such status.

We noticed some gender divides also – men and women engage in different literacy practices. There were class and occupational divides also; poor farmers engaged in different literacy from the richer tradesmen; the women in the markets used different numeracies from their wholesalers.

6. We came to the conclusion that all of these are valid forms of literacy and numeracy, that they are different and equally valid. For we noted that each of them had their own functionality. Rather than 'functionality' being tied to only one form of literacy and numeracy, that taught in 'Functional Literacy Programmes', we saw the informal literacies of the shopkeepers as very functional for their

purposes. Religious literacies had functionality for religious rituals and for membership of a religious 'community of practice', but it did not have a functionality for reading a newspaper or writing a letter. The schooled literacy has a functionality for continuing in education and for getting a job in the formal economic sector, but it does not help anyone to read the Qu'ran or a *sura* or for the informal literacies of the marketplace. Each literacy and numeracy has its own value in its own context.

7. For this reason, we felt that in our adult literacy learning programmes, we should try to bring the various kinds of literacy and numeracy together. We came to see that, because the literacy practices of the classroom are different from the literacy and numeracy practices of the home, the market, the community, there is a barrier to the learners learning the classroom literacy practices and especially to them taking these formal literacy practices into their daily lives.

We decided that starting with the more informal local literacy practices before moving on to the formal school literacy practices will help the learners to make sense of their literacies and more easily to relate their literacy learning to their daily lives. We also agreed that adding the schooled literacy practices of the classroom to the local literacies would increase the range of skills available to those who came to learn – they would be able to cope with new sets of literacy and numeracy practices. And we could use these existing local literacy and numeracy practices in helping our learners to learn the formal literacy of the school.

> *We aim to bring the local literacy and numeracy practices into the classroom and the classroom literacy and numeracy practices out into the community.*

8. We came to agree that learning literacy and numeracy are not enough to bring social and economic benefits, to help people get out of poverty; that they need to **use them in their daily lives**. So our concern is to identify the special uses of the local literacies and to encourage and enable the learners first to learn them and secondly to use these in their daily lives, and then move them on to the formal schooled literacy and numeracy taught in the adult

classroom. We came to realise that teaching a core' literacy to be used later in life would not be so useful or practicable as building on the existing literacy and numeracy practices which the learners already have. We aim to teach literacy and numeracy practices that are embedded in real life situations rather than a detached 'literacy' and 'numeracy'.

> *Literacy is learned to be used. The benefits come from using literacy, not from learning literacy – i.e. from literacy and numeracy practices rather than from 'literacy' or 'numeracy'.*

Learning the formal literacy and numeracy practices of the classroom will become easier if the informal literacy and numeracy practices of the everyday can be valued by the facilitators, brought into the classroom and related to the formal practices. Bringing their own everyday matters into the classroom will help the learners to see the relevance of what they are learning to their daily lives. This should make the learning much easier and more motivating for the learners who will quickly be able to see the connection between their literacy learning and their everyday life and to continue learning even when not interacting with the literacy facilitators.

9. This is in line with the general principles on which adult learning programmes are built. Adult facilitators are always trained (as we saw in a review of training manuals for facilitators which we conducted during the workshop) that teaching adult learners is different from teaching children because adults bring to their classrooms much existing knowledge and experience and they are already engaged in many (literacy and especially numeracy) practices. Those who teach adults should 'start where they [the learners] are', build on their existing practices, use their existing knowledge and experience in the classroom.

> *Start from where the learners are, from what they know and do.*

10. It is this which led us to develop ethnographic approaches to adult literacy and numeracy. For in this approach, the facilitators will need to try to find out what their learners know, what they have experienced, how they see the world, what they are doing in their daily lives and livelihood activities, and how literacy is involved in these activities.

And to do that they need to use ethnographic approaches. As we have seen above, traditional research methods such as asking the learners on their own will not result in full knowledge of what the learners are doing in literacy and numeracy. In many cases, the learners will not really know what they are doing, for they are often unconscious of such practices. Or they will not regard the 'scrappy' writing or calculating they are doing as 'literacy' or 'numeracy'; it is not the 'right' kind of activity. Or they may tell us what they feel we want to know. Only a mixture of observing, asking and analysing will lead to an appreciation of these practices and the value attached to them.

> *How can we find out where they are? What they do?*
>
> **One answer is ethnographic-style study or research**

Other findings from our case studies and fieldwork

Before looking at how we can use these local literacies and numeracies in helping adults to learn the standardised formal literacy of the classroom, we examined some of the other findings from our fieldwork and case studies which might be of value in our work. We have chosen here some of the things which struck us as being new, which opened our eyes. The case studies are full of the word 'surprised', for we found our own assumptions were constantly being challenged.

Focusing on the daily lives as a whole

The case studies placed a strong emphasis on **traditional methods** of doing things (e.g. counting, measuring, etc). But equally we were aware that ethnography is not about traditional ways of doing things, neither is it about informal ways only but rather about all the existing popular ways of life, that is, life as it is being lived by the community under study. There is in much ethnography of literacy and numeracy a tendency to ignore what appears to be formal and concentrate on what is seen as traditional and informal ways of doing things. The case studies here have also been influenced by this perception of ethnography, hence their emphasis on informal and traditional methods of counting etc, sometimes not seeing the formal methods also in use in the community.

For example, we noticed in one field visit that a vaccination card for a child that was carefully wrapped in a polythene paper and hung on a wall was ignored, while the participants were more interested in the stones which a shopkeeper had improvised as weights for his weighing scale and the different glasses that the same woman with the child vaccination card was using as measures for selling her local brews etc. If these vaccination cards are among the important written materials that the community is confronted with on a daily basis and thus constitutes part of their literacies, they cannot be ignored just because they are formal and come from a formal health institution. An ethnography of literacy in any community does not concentrate solely on the non-literate and on the specifically local literacy and numeracy practices but on all the practices, formal and informal.

Occupations: we found far more people engaged in working their own way out of poverty than we expected. We did not choose these case studies because they were engaged in income generation activities; but the range of different livelihoods which presented themselves to us was striking. Most of them were individual but in some cases they formed partnerships as in the case of Hambelle and Guye – and if (as in the case of Mulu the farmer's wife and her aunt) the partnership did not work, they broke up and went on, on their own.

In particular, We did not expect them, especially the women, to be engaged in multiple occupations. Genet "is fighting poverty by engaging himself in different activities. He is working as a daily labourer obtaining 15 to 20 birr per day besides farming. He told us he and all participants in the FAL centre took practical lessons on nursery growing, which helped them to cultivate and sell plants for people who want to plant in their land. Now he is preparing seedlings of eucalyptus trees and green peppers to sell in the coming summer." "Currently she [Enani] is engaged in a number of small business activities such as poultry and sheep farming, and her husband works on cattle fattening." Abate the house builder said that working in the butchery is one of his part-time activities. Mulu the farmer's wife fattened oxen and brewed arakie. Hambelle and Guye told us: "We have different activities like araki making, tella, buying clothes, and retailing, etc., because if one fails to be profitable, the others will compensate; for example, if banana retailing costs decrease, we get income from araki or others." Guyato brewed drinks and fattened sheep.

And they changed their occupations as and when changes in the local economy and the seasons made it worthwhile to do so, carefully working out reasons for this change. Enani started in grain, turned over to araki, then to *tella* brewing and finally to making and selling bread with her drinks. She went on:

> "The other activity we were engaged in was poultry some time ago. But an epidemic erupted, killing a large number of hens in the village. We sold our chickens at low prices so as not to be a victim of the epidemic. Though we were taught on modern poultry and the vaccination for disease prevention, we found it very laborious and costly. Moreover, fodder for the chicken is not easily available. It requires investing huge money compared to arakie preparation. Distillation and selling arakie is relatively simple and less costly". She added, "Poultry need additional manpower that stays around when we are away from the house."

Here are reflexive traders. They made a serious study of their chosen occupations. They asked around; they watched for some days other traders in the market. Efe said that in the course of time, she was forced to change her tray and basket making to selling vegetables, as sitting for long hours to produce the traditional trays coupled with continuous giving birth to 8 children (6 girls and a boy, one died at an early age) caused her to have backache. She also compared the profit gained and the time spent to produce the traditional trays and the money gained from the sale of vegetables. *"It takes some days to produce local trays and I get only two birr profit, whereas I get more than two birr profit a day from selling vegetables."* Ade similarly decided to change from making arakie because she felt she was losing money. "After thinking thoroughly, she went to market to observe the work her relatives do. Her relatives buy different kinds of grains from the farmers or wholesalers and resell to consumers. Observing this, after a week she decided to start this work specialising a little bit. Ade Yeshi buys different kinds of grains as her relatives do. But she mixes them. After mixing, she sells using the same measurement that she uses for buying." She did not copy; she made her own niche in the grain market.

We noticed that in our case studies, few of them were using any literacy or written numeracy practices in their livelihood activities. Even those who possessed literacy skills felt that it was enough to keep their accounts 'in their heads'. This led to a major challenge to us. All our literacy learning programmes so far have concentrated on the people defined as 'illiterate'; but we can also focus on helping those who do possess literacy skills to see how they can use these more effectively in their daily life activities.

One thing which struck us was that the women, none of whom kept written records, were running two different systems of accounts in their head at the same time. There was the 'normal' approach which appears in the textbooks – that is, to determine the income first: how much do we have to spend? to be followed by expenditure second, what can we afford to buy? This was the way they ran their household expenditure – they had a certain sum available to them and therefore they could afford to buy this thing but not to buy that thing. But in their livelihood activities, their accounting system was different. They all told us first what they had spent – that is, they started with the expenditure. Then they calculated what they would have to charge to make sure that they more than covered their expenditure. This process is not taught in any of the textbooks. But they were managing the two systems without any sense of contradiction, any sense of difficulty. They switched unconsciously between the two systems effortlessly.

Empowerment of 'illiterate women': We found men and especially women who were in control of their lives. They had problems and poverty; but even Wudnesh who had lost money through her borrowings had taken charge and built a new future for herself. Here are women who plan their futures for themselves and especially for their children and grandchildren: "I am taking a contraceptive not to have a child. Sometime in the future we have a plan to have one or two children." Enani and her husband plan to send their children to school in the next year. "We have dreams of improving our families' economic well-being, developing our own income-generating project, setting our children, especially our daughters, on a path to a better life through school and even university which they never dreamed of for themselves". "Why do you focus on your daughter?" "Because I don't want her to live my life". Because I did not have an education myself, I am sending my children to school, said Asha the weaver: "I had no schooling. I did not go to any school, my father did not send me to any school, for he was non–literate and wanted my labour at that time." Asha continued saying, "This reminds me of something. You know , when I grew older, I decided to get married and be blessed with children. After eight years, I got married and currently I am the father of three kids. I started sending my kids to school. This year I sent my daughter to one of the private schools, she is learning at grade 1 and my son to the kindergarten level one, to take revenge against my no schooling."

Here are men and especially women who manage their own development. They receive training from health extension workers and livelihood trainers. "The health extension worker, Zenebech, has taught us how to keep our house clean and where to dispose of garbage and dirt. She also taught us that we get ill if we don't keep ourselves clean." Ayelech thoughtfully manages her mosquito nets because of her training. Enani attended a training programme which gave her an insight to expand her poultry, and she like several of the others is a member of a literacy-led savings and credit programme. And Genet the farmer claimed proudly, "We built a toilet and use it properly; that is important to prevent contaminated diseases. We constructed a fuel-saving stove, a mud shelf for household utensils, and a ground well for dry waste disposal." Illiteracy was no bar to these people's determination to improve their own lives. They are in their own ways already empowered.

Learning: We would like to have explored their out-of-school ways of learning in greater depth. We noticed many learning through the family: as Asha said, "I used to help my father while he was weaving. I learned weaving skills from him … This is a practice which I acquired from my father." Guyato learned her method of accounting from her father describing her grandfather's methods of counting cattle: "I think it is my grandfather's experience that was transferred to me and helps me to calculate my loan of return". But not just their immediate family of parents and grandparents, although they were important, but other relatives – aunts and cousins. "I had no experience on how to prepare it, I didn't have a mother to show me how to prepare it either. While I was thinking, an idea came to my mind, consulting my aunt". But perhaps the most important were their neighbours, especially through the coffee ceremony which is such a feature of the different parts of the country they came from. Many picked up new ideas and learned the skills they needed from neighbours during the coffee ceremony. In one of our case studies, some of the neighbours had learned a wide range of things from an 'illiterate' woman. Hambelle and Guye started their trading after discussion at the coffee ceremony, as did Guyato. They learned from friends, from their whole social environment.: "A friend of hers in the market who sells cheese and butter introduced Efe to this business activity". "I really want to appreciate those people who have continuously coached, mentored and supervised my construction works and enabled me to be a good constructor of residential as well as business/commercial houses". Almaz the domestic servant learned from her whole social environment: "I also learned many things in the house I was working with, particularly when relatives were chatting during festivals." And they learned on the job: "Abate started working as a daily labourer providing assistance to a local carpenter and a traditional house contractor by carrying and delivering tools to them. His assignment was only on a daily basis, as he did not possess practical experience in the field of carpentry or construction. It took him quite a lot of time and many difficult moments to reach a level of perfection". Our case studies taught us that the 'illiterate' learners who come to adult literacy learning programmes are already learning in a number of different ways and they bring these multiple ways of learning with them – they do not have to be taught how to learn!

And on the whole, this group of case studies held positive attitudes towards formal schooling. Enani sought by every means to avoid the abduction route to marriage for the sake of her schooling but in the end her career was interrupted, preventing her from benefitting fully from schooling. Asha the weaver sent his children to private school, vividly saying it was a revenge for him not having schooling himself. Abate the builder-butcher had more ambivalent feelings towards school: "having attended the formal education up to grade 9 has helped me, but none of the skills I am currently using are from the schools. All of my works are up to the standard, both in a butchery or and in the field of construction."

Religion: Finally, we came to appreciate the important role that religion played in the daily lives of these people. They swore oaths of loyalty on the church; they made decisions about amounts of money to commit to enterprises according to saint's days; they relied on the interventions of the saints to keep their money safe. They counted dates by religious festivals and calculated ages through the church. Enani brought a monk into the conversation. Ayelech put a cross into her pictures to denote her religion and the sanctity of marriage; and could recognise pictures of the Virgin Mary and Child while denying that her pictures possessed any virtue of representation in this respect. Any adult learning programme for people such as these which omitted all mention of religion would hardly connect with the daily lives of the learners.

There are many other aspects of life which these case studies reveal and each of us will find things which strike us most. But the importance of these findings for our work as adult educators has still to be examined. Having found out what their learners are doing in the way of local literacy and numeracy practices and in other aspects of their lives, how then should the facilitators use these findings in the classroom? How can they relate to the learning programme already provided by the literacy programme? What are the major implications of our ethnographic studies? The workshop turned to this issue next.

Implications for adult literacy learning programmes

Creating or adapting a curriculum? Before we started on this consideration however, the workshop participants turned to discussing their own situation. During the discussions on how to use the findings of ethnographic research in our adult learning programmes, a distinction was identified between those participants who felt themselves to be able to develop new learning programmes, new curricula and new teaching-learning materials and those who felt that they are obliged to teach to a pre-ordained programme using set textbooks. It was agreed that we need a model which could be used by both groups of programmes. Some of us, especially those who worked in or with government institutions and educational institutions, felt that they had very limited room for manoeuvre; they and their facilitators are tied to a set curriculum, a set primer and other materials, and a set examination. Others, mainly those working with NGOs, still felt that they could experiment with devising a completely new curriculum, able to create completely new programmes with a new curriculum and new teaching-learning materials. Nirantar (as we shall see) was creating a completely new form of adult learning programme in a participatory way, getting learners as well as facilitators to work with them in developing new aims and objectives, activities, materials and forms of assessment – but not all of us have that freedom or the resources to do that in such detail.

But it was agreed that all facilitators, whatever their programme, were able to supplement their existing programmes by bringing in additional subject matter and use additional teaching-learning materials developed from their ethnographic studies and materials which come from the learners. We agreed that there is always room and time available in any adult literacy programme for the facilitator to bring in additional material from the learners. For what we were looking for was a new attitude of the facilitator to the learners – not to regard them as ignorant and inexperienced in literacy and numeracy but to seek out what they know and especially what they are already doing bit by bit and to help the learners to build on that. That can be done even within the tightest existing curriculum.

A new approach to adult learners

The first conclusion then which applies to teachers of adults in both situations is that this implies a changed role for the teacher of adults, a changed set of relationships within the class, a changed attitude towards the learner. For when one looks at what the adult learners are already doing in their lives, we realised that it will be impossible to continue to regard the learners who come to adult literacy learning programmes as 'illiterate' – as ignorant, as having nothing to contribute to the programme, as having no control over their own learning, as lacking in confidence.

And if we can no longer regard the learners as 'illiterate', perhaps the justification for having classes which are exclusively confined to 'illiterates' needs to be thought about again. Since adults tend to learn best from their family and neighbours, it may be useful to form mixed groups of literate and 'illiterate' to share their learning.

We found men and women who had considerable control over their lives, who were making forward steps in their own ways, self-reliant. We found men and women who were learning – and learning quickly. They used many strategies for their own learning – from family and neighbours, from trial and error, from the churches and mosques, from discussion in small groups. Adults learn a great deal from other adults, more than from a teacher, which suggests much for our formal adult learning programmes. Collaborative rather than individualised learning is the norm in everyday learning, and the learners in our adult learning programmes could perhaps learn more effectively from each other than from the facilitator. They are used to learning in that way.

We found men and women who controlled their own finances, articulate and confident, who expressed their feelings strongly, who did not feel they needed help, who taught us a great deal when we met them. And yet when these same men and women come into our adult literacy learning programmes, they change their identities: they become meek, unconfident, reliant on the teacher, conscious of their lack of everything. The purpose of our adult learning programmes must surely be to help the learners to realise who they really are, to recognise their own large funds of knowledge, to value their own practices as well as to learn more. What our programmes are doing is to 'add value', not to teach ignorant and unskilful people what they do not know and what they cannot do.

The changed attitude of the programme planners and the facilitators to the adults who come to us to learn new things will be the greatest result of our ethnographic studies of local literacy and numeracy practices.

One way of achieving this new attitude, and of showing that we appreciate the value of what the learners know and do, is to use these same funds of knowledge and practices in our teaching-learning programmes, The workshop looked at this question in some detail. Our aim is that our facilitators should build on the existing experience of the learners, on their tacit funds of knowledge and on their existing practices. To bring adults into a classroom and to ignore what they already do and teach them some new thing is to treat them like children, not as adults. It is to erect barriers to effective learning – barriers of our making, not theirs.

This is widely recognised in other sectors of development education. Agricultural extension workers, for example, always start off assuming that the learners are already farming and seek to build on these existing practices and help the farmers to change and improve. The same is true of fishing communities – no-one brings in fishermen and tries to teach them about fishing in their own location, or the fishermen would walk out! Even in health extension, many workers in nutrition will start by asking the women they teach about their families' existing eating, shopping and cooking habits. They all build on what the learners know and do.

One suggested barrier to such an approach was considered. Some have suggested that adults – like children – need to learn simple words first and then move to more complicated words. But ethnographic research shows that adults do not learn in this way. Rather they move from the known to the unknown. They learn what appear to others as difficult words if these are words they use regularly and which mean a great deal to them. Adults can learn from the texts they find around them; they do not need to use specially prepared texts as if they were children.

The workshop participants then sought to find a way in which this approach can be developed in relation to literacy and numeracy. Our researches had shown that even so-called 'illiterate' people engage in literacy and especially in numeracy tasks. They may use mediators such as their children to read something or write a list or accounts. They adopt different strategies; and they often can do much more than we or they think they can do. Our task is to find out these existing practices, and the beliefs and values they are based on, and to try to find ways in which to use them in our classroom activities.

What then we seek are ways to help facilitators to become 'researchers', to be able to survey the existing literacy and numeracy practices of their learners and the community from which they come. And this is best done with the learners – not regarding the learners as the 'object' of research but as co-researchers. The learners can teach us a great deal about their own daily lives and the role that literacy and numeracy plays in that life world. In this way, we can help the learners to reflect critically on their own experiences of literacy and numeracy.

And having researched and discovered much about the experiences of literacy and numeracy that their learners already have, the facilitators need to be encouraged to use these findings in their teaching. As Nirantar has discovered, it is likely that most facilitators will be relatively good at collecting information, but they may be less able to use this information, to include their findings in their daily teaching and learning programmes unless they are given substantial training and a good deal of technical support.

The Nirantar model

In this stage of our studies, we were greatly helped by the work done in India by Nirantar as described in the workshop by Malini Ghose.

The objectives which Nirantar set before themselves when developing a new programme for the *dalit* women in Uttar Pradesh with whom they were working were to enable the women to *read* their environment (mapping the literate environment), to bring 'texts' from the environment into the classroom, to enable the women to use literacy and numeracy in their contexts, and to bring literacy and numeracy together, not to separate them. The whole aim of the programme (as Malini put it) is to interrogate the power relations within which the reading of these texts are embedded, in terms of, for example, gender and the divide between literate and illiterate (see Nirantar 2007).

'Calendars' were chosen as one major theme, as the ethnographic research found calendars in most homes and also found this an interesting subject which Nirantar and the women themselves felt could be developed further. A joint research team of Nirantar staff, facilitators and some learners researched and collected calendars from the participants and from the community.

On a pilot basis, the team set out to use the research findings and observations to develop teaching-learning material, involving facilitators and programme staff in the process of material development (it became a form of hands-on training). The next stage was to see how this material could then be used to train facilitators for wider dissemination. This work is still in progress.

Researching calendars revealed that reading calendars is not a part of the everyday practices of people, although most houses have an 'English calendar' which is referred to for dates of bank repayments, court hearings, etc. The local priest is consulted for dates of festivals, for example, and auspicious dates, etc but the religious calendar (*'panchang'*) is expensive. Only a few people have it in their houses.

It was found that many women can read the numbers but cannot decipher the calendar matrix. It was also found that there are local ways of tracking dates, for example tracking dates through the moon cycle. Each day of the moon cycle has a particular name.

The team decided to explore further some areas which needed fuller discussion., such as whether the women in the programme wanted to learn to read calendars, how they track time locally, how the local system interfaces with the standard calendar, and what are the practices and power relations which accessing calendars is embedded in. The group agreed that the facilitators could help them to explore these issues further and in the material development process itself.

The development of the new learning programme was undertaken by setting up a small group who would take this forward - 4 facilitators, 1 co-ordinator and 2 staff from Nirantar who met in a series of participatory workshops, followed by field-testing at selected centres and camps. The group engaged in collective reflection, using detailed field notes which they compiled, leading to further refinement and additions to the learning programme. The group agreed that the approach they would follow would be to begin with the learners 'funds of knowledge' and experiences and to build on that, to engage with that experience through dialogue and discussion, bringing in new ideas. In this way, they were seeking to teach and strengthen/reinforce literacy and numeracy.

The first workshop was characterised by free-flowing brainstorming. Its contents included collecting local ways of tracking dates, of making connections between the lunar and solar calendars, and of reading the calendar - numbers, names of the weekdays and months. Issues around the concept of time, day and night and the seasons led to information about daily and seasonal work patterns, including issues around the gender division of labour.

This material was then organised into four main themes:

1. Understanding local ways of tracking dates compared with 'standard' calendars.

2. Day and night, seasons.

3. Calendars and women's work.

4. Different types of calendars (religious).

A pattern of working towards new teaching-learning material was developed as follows:

Theme	Existing Funds of knowledge	New ideas	Literacy and Numeracy activities (E.G. Worksheets)

Each theme was developed into learning sessions, and worksheets for literacy and numeracy were created.

To give one example from Theme 1: Understanding local ways of tracking dates, collecting the information found that the women track dates based on the phases of the moon from one full moon to no moon, and from no moon to full moon. So activities were designed where the women named each day in their local language, linked this visually to the phase of the moon, and then used these to develop their own calendars. The lunar and solar calendars were linked and compared. The women were taught to read locally available calendars, mentioning both systems but not before they made sense of calendars on their own. They learned to write the days of the week. Puzzles around the calendar were developed. The women learnt to write the names of the months in the local language (Bundeli) and then in Hindi and English. As the moon was central to this work, the Nirantar staff asked them to tell and write local stories, songs or idioms about the moon.

It is important to note that Nirantar encouraged the women to write as they pleased, which helped break fears around writing correctly. They report that it was exciting to see women who are often reluctant to engage with the written word trying to write and asking for help to spell 'correctly'.

Discussion found that access to calendars was not equal between men and women and between the educated and the non-literate. Despite being interested, women never think of using calendars themselves. In addition, even if they know how to use them, they never think of reading a calendar hanging in a public space and using it. Placing the calendar in women's hands helped to demystify it. The women later remarked, "*Now we know we can touch it. It is also meant for us. It is not so alien.*"

Discussion of the religious calendars revealed that different festivals are celebrated in different seasons; the women looked for the red markings on the calendar. They discussed how and why different festivals are celebrated. In addition, they asked 'why?' As Nirantar commented, we all tend to know so little about festivals in other communities. Many myths and perceptions of 'the other' were discussed.

Malini's presentation ended with a list of challenges which they were still facing - how to help the facilitators to deal with the interface between different systems of knowledge, and how to keep coming back to learners' experiences; how to deal with a mixed group in terms of interests and literacy/numeracy needs; how to link literacy with the other content. And there was the issue of assessment – how to measure the 'uses of literacy', the changes in behaviour which resulted from the programme.

A worksheet from Theme 1

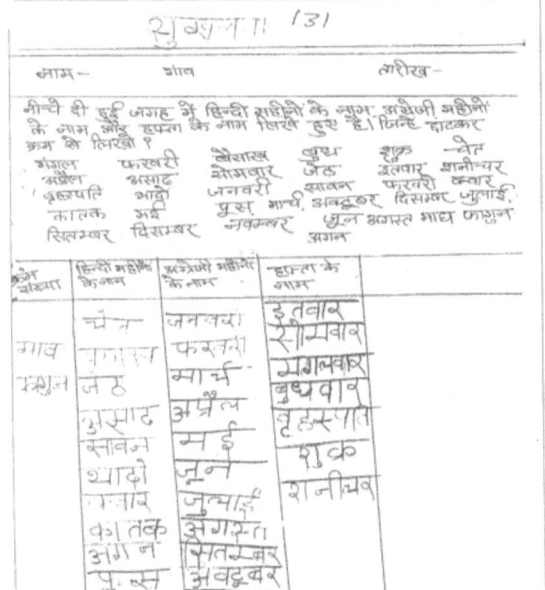

A worksheet from Theme 4

Using the findings in the adult classroom

Based on this example of ways of using the findings in teaching adults, the workshop participants came up with a general model of how facilitators could use the findings of ethnographic research in their adult literacy classes.

We wanted a model which would apply to any topic which was selected by the facilitator, in consultation with the learners, based on the findings of the ethnographic research. These topics will come from the ethnographic research. In new programmes which are being fully developed, such topics can come up from discussion of the findings of the research with the learners. In other programmes, the topic will often be suggested by the textbook, but that will still allow the facilitator space to identify local practices which can support what he/she is teaching. When teaching maths, for example, receipts can provide supplementary examples of maths being used in the community.

The CRB approach

Through extensive discussion, the following model was developed for the process of developing a teaching-learning programme which uses the learners' existing knowledge and practices. It was intended to be a new pattern of adult learning programme which can be fitted either within an existing curriculum or used to develop a new approach completely. We called it the 'CRB approach', for it is built on three elements:

Collect (discover): For every topic being covered in the course, the facilitator will collect the existing practices and funds of knowledge and the different local literacies from the community as much as possible through visits, observation, interviews, meeting with people both formally and informally.

In this process, the learners can help the facilitator. This may be hard at first – they may not be used to being consulted. Their picture of themselves may be that they have nothing to contribute to the school learning process. But it is possible to discover from them orally and by observation what are their experience, their ideas, their knowledge, and especially their practices. Collecting this will reveal that the facilitator values and respects the learners, indeed has something to learn from them. It will change the learners' thinking about themselves and they will come to learn more quickly and more deeply. Their confidence will be built up.

Reflect (discuss): Once the materials have been collected, the learning group of facilitator and learners together can reflect on these local practices, the texts and practices which have been found in the local community. This will consist of a deliberate programme of discussing this collected material with them freely, getting them to reflect on it, whether it is just, whether it can be improved. How texts are used in the community, including gender and power issues, what are the literacy and numeracy practices involved in them, who uses them and who created them (and for what purpose), how they are using them, who is excluded from using them and how and why they are excluded – all these are issues which the learners can explore. In this way, a sense of desire for change can be developed and enhanced.

This stage of reflection is very important. It has often been recommended that 'real materials' should be collected from the community, bringing texts in from environment and using them to supplement or even to replace the textbook (Rogers 1999), and this is being done in a number of programmes. But such texts are treated as if they were a textbook – they are decontextualised, words are taken out of their sentences and broken up and through the learning of the individual elements (letters and syllables), new (equally decontextualised) words are created. But this is not the approach of LETTER, for here we are studying not texts, even when drawn from the community, but literacy practices – how texts are produced in the local community, how they are used and by whom, what they mean to those who made them and to those who possess them. So, after the collection of literacy and numeracy materials from the community, the learning group will engage on this process of Reflection, in-depth discussion and exploration of these materials in their specific context.

Build on (develop): During such discussions, the facilitator will seek to build on what has been learned from this sharing process, to introduce new ideas and information, new skills (especially new forms of literacy and numeracy practices), new ways of working. New kinds of learning activities, new forms of writing and new ways of calculating including written forms can be developed. The facilitator does not need to stay only with the textbook and the teachers' manual; he/she can develop additional activities for the learners to do, using their existing knowledge and practices as the basis for new learning. By building on what the learners bring to the class, the new learning is now firmly attached to the everyday life of the learners and it will in consequence be taken back into the community at the end of each lesson. It will be seen to be relevant to their existing practices.

We felt that it is important not to see these as three separate stages; rather they are elements which will be intertwined throughout the learning session. While discussing the topic in depth, new knowledge can be provided; when reflecting, some writing and some numeracy activities can be incorporated. This can be done even within existing programmes. Every lesson has a topic; the learners can be encouraged to *contribute* from their existing knowledge and especially their existing practices. This material they have provided (orally in most cases but sometimes with texts from the community) can then be *discussed*; and during the discussion, *new learning activities* can be built in.

The participants in the workshop agreed that, while developing themes for learning, we need to keep in mind the following questions:

- Where are they (i.e. the learners)? - the "start where they are" principle of adult education

- Where do they want to go? Where do we want to take them?

- How can we help them to get there, using their existing practices and their funds of knowledge?

- How will we build on their knowledge? Where will they practise their knowledge?

Training the facilitators in the 'CRB approach' is simply another way of putting that part of all facilitator training which is concerned with 'adult learning'. Simply telling facilitators that adult learners bring knowledge and experience with them to the class does not help them to discover this knowledge and the practices which they do. We can train them to

- Collect the existing knowledge and practices from their learners and from the community

- Reflect together on these practices

- Build on this knowledge and these practices.

Some of the LETTER workshop group suggested we list these three activities as

Discover

Discuss

Develop.

If you find it more helpful to remember the three 'd's, then use whichever you wish; but the workshop participants agreed that in future they will do what they can to ensure that their facilitators build on what the learners already do (which they can find out by using an ethnographic approach) and not just ignore this. For rejecting what the learners do, what they value, and what they know, is to reject the learner. And that will prevent real learning.

Some learning themes from the case studies

The participants were surprised at the large number of findings which they saw could be used in the formal adult literacy classes. Among these were the following:

- Receipts: Many of the livelihood activities involved giving or receiving of written receipts. Learning to write and read these could form a useful activity

- Counting: The participants were stuck by the many different ways in which the people in the case studies counted (this is discussed more fully below)

- Measurements: Again we found many different ways of measuring – time, distance, weights, volume, space, etc

- Communication: The learners will bring with them different ways in which they communicate, from written words (personal letter writing and small notes) to signs, from cellphones to paintings on the wall of their houses. The group noted that oral transmission of information and other systems of storage and transfers such as memorisation were being used by the local community. Since a large part of the functionality of every literacy is communication, discussion of these alternative ways of communicating will lead to an appreciation of the values of literacy in communication.

- Proverbs and sayings: We found several examples of these (for fuller discussion, see below).

- **Stories** told among members of the communities – the learners will all have their own stories.

- Income and expenditure: The livelihood activities we discovered undertaken by those who are regarded as 'literate' and 'illiterate' are based on different ways of raising and spending income (again, we shall discuss this in more detail below)

- Profit and loss: Working out profit and loss means calculating in some form or other their expenditure and income. Most of our case studies did this mentally rather than in writing. The different ways in which the adult learners already do this can be taken and used in the class rather than just one model given to the learners as the right way to keep their accounts. We felt that starting with a generic model of 'keeping accounts' and applying that to their different activities (in effect trying to force their own accounting systems into a strait-jacket of a textbook model of accounting) would not be as effective as starting with their different ways of reckoning and improving on these.

- Savings: Some of the adult learners will have different attitudes towards savings and savings schemes, based on their experiences. An examination of the different ways the community use to record their saving can became the basis for learning much literacy and numeracy.

- Loans: Similarly for loans

- Helping others: We noticed how many of our participants were engaged in sharing, in helping others

- Pictures: Some of our case studies involved people creating their own pictures. Not only is this a skill which can be used in the classroom, but discussion on who produces such pictures, for what purpose; who reads them, how useful are they – including gender dimensions – can be very useful for helping the learners to see the relevance of what they are learning to their own communities.

- Poems and songs: Like stories, the learners will have their own favourite songs and common poems. Collecting these from the learners and writing them down; helping the learners to read them and write more will create an exciting learning environment for both learners and facilitator.

- Timings: Finding out how people who do not have watches calculate time can provide much food for discussion and for learning new skills including much literacy and numeracy.

- Negotiation: As with helping others and sharing, we found many of our case study respondents engaged in negotiation – with traders, with neighbours, etc. Again we felt this could be used for further learning.

Following discussion, we came to the conclusion that we want to teach literacy and numeracy practices which will be of relevance to the learners – not to teach a common core 'literacy' and a decontextualised 'numeracy' which can be applied later but (using basic adult education approaches of learning by doing rather than learning for future doing) to teach literacy and numeracy practices which are of immediate usefulness to the learners, practices which come from their own community activities.

Four examples of developing learning programmes from ethnographic findings

At the participants' request, a few themes were discussed in some depth so that, in small groups, they could develop some ideas of how to build a learning programme around an identified theme. The workshop thus decided to take four themes to see how it could work out – four themes drawn from the case studies in this book. The themes they chose were as follows:

1. Counting

2. Measuring

3. Income and expenditure (calculating profit)

4. Proverbs, songs and poems

Counting

The workshop participants noticed that the case studies showed people, both those officially 'illiterate' and literate, using many different ways of counting – by the use of people's ages, by selected dates. One used maize seeds, another the buttons on his coat. One had an elaborate system of using sticks which showed that she had worked out for herself the 'place value' of formal mathematics – that two sticks changed their value according to the place they were put on the ground; in one place, they represented 'two', but in another place, they represented 'twenty'. Several used fingers (and one their toes as well), but this did not mean they all counted in units of five and ten – some counted three to a finger giving a different base unit.

The situations in which they count clearly influence how they do it. In religious contexts, counting (dates, for example) may be different for them from dealing with money. Counting sheep again may be different. Valuing the different ways in which counting is done in the communities from which the learners come will completely change a lesson on counting from one in which the facilitator simply teaches what is in the primer and tries to get the learners to adopt a completely new (to them) process.

Collecting together such examples can lead to a number of conclusions. First, we do not need to teach adults to count – they already count, often to high numbers (one informant claimed he could count in his head up to three thousand). We need to discover how they count and to value that as a different (not necessarily inferior) way of counting.

This can lead to a discussion among the learners (through reflection) about the differences between these methods. Do women tend to count in different ways from men? Do schooled people count differently from unschooled? There will always be a tendency to believe that the schooled form of counting, using a base of ten, is the 'right' way to count, that all other approaches are incorrect or liable to more error. But different people have adopted different styles of counting for different purposes.

During such discussions, new ways of counting can be introduced. This will not replace their existing ways of counting by asserting that this is the 'right' way to count; rather it will build on them. Our aim is to help the learners to learn new ways so that they can increase the choice available to them.

Measuring

We found that there are in every community we visited different ways of measuring solid and liquid volumes, lengths etc. Local names are given to the various measuring devices, and these are known and accepted. What is often taught in the classroom is only a very limited range of measuring tools (kilograms, litres, metres). There are many more ways of measuring than these and some people may be much happier using their normal modes of measuring than changing to ours. What is more, we found our informants switching happily and frequently between one mode and another – buying in kilograms and selling in cupfuls, for example. Thirdly, we found a great deal was done by approximation, by estimation – weighing butter by the hand, for example.

Collecting different ways of measuring, reflecting on these in depth, discussing them in the classroom, would lead to a great deal of strongly held views about the value or limitations of different ways of measuring being challenged. Again, is there a gender dimension to this? Certainly different measurements are used for different tasks and in different contexts. And such discussions can be used to build new ways of measuring using standardised measures, so that the range of ways available to the learners is increased.

To teach measuring in the classroom from a textbook without collecting in first the ways in which the learners are already measuring is surely to court disaster – there will be little effective learning. But the existing measuring practices can be built upon; new ways can be acquired by the learners so long as they are related to the existing practices.

Income and expenditure

Collecting the experiences which the case studies presented to us in terms of income generation and the calculation of profit from trading and production enabled us to identify another area which can be used in adult learning programmes. Many of our researchers asked the informants how they kept records of their expenditure and incomes.

Reflecting: When we came to discuss the various livelihood case studies we had collected, we noticed a number of features, some of which surprised us. First, as we have seen above, many, if not most, of those we met were engaged in multiple occupations, not just one income generation activity. The rationale for this was clearly stated – they could control their own incomes more effectively if they could switch between occupations to suit the market. These women did not need training in income generation; indeed, they could teach others a good deal. But there were ways in which their activities could be improved.

One way was the application of literacy to their livelihoods. None of those who had learned literacy skills used any of these skills for their occupations; they still kept accounts in their head. Those who came to adult literacy learning programmes came for the livelihood skills training on offer, not for the literacy.

We noticed two other features of these income generation activities. One was the general issue of secrecy – keeping such activities and the income derived from them secret from other members of the family, especially the husband. This must give rise to extensive discussions in the class of gender issues. Secondly, we noted the strong element of religion in their decision-making – swearing on the church door, choosing religious dates to determine how much to borrow, etc. To ignore such elements in the learning programmes is to ignore a very wide ranging part of the lives of the learners; to respect this is to respect the learners.

Many adult literacy and numeracy learning programmes include a section on keeping accounts as part of the learning curriculum. Apart from the issue of different processes of calculating their accounts which we have noticed above, when we looked at the ways in which the people in our case studies managed their accounts, and especially how they calculated their profit, we noticed in particular one feature. Most of them were very good at calculating profits mentally but only in strictly cash terms; they tended to omit the 'intangibles', those unsubstantial elements such as the time involved and their own labour costs. Mentally, they simply balanced money spent against money gained - and a small margin was satisfactory to them. Conducting these same accounts on paper enabled them to include the missing elements more easily.

Collecting these examples of income and expenditure will enable a full discussion (reflection) of many aspects of profit making; and will provide a more relevant context in which the learners can build new ideas, new practices, can learn written (and more comprehensive) forms of accounting. Using their real-life examples will demonstrate the relevance of the new learning to their activities and will provide motivation for changing their practices. The use of literacy in livelihoods can be promoted only if the facilitator is able to use the real-life income-generation activities of the learners as teaching-learning materials and give them precise examples of how literacy practices can fit their existing economic activities.

Proverbs, songs and poems

The group decided there were enough examples of proverbs and other sayings which could be used in adult literacy classes. Many came from the community itself, written on the walls. **Collecting** such sayings from the learners and from the walls of the community is fairly easy. The learners can be sent out with their notebooks to copy what they see and bring it into the class – even if they cannot 'read' it. Other proverbs and poems can be collected orally from the learners and written down by the facilitator. Songs too – traditional folk songs, or film and TV songs – can also be collected and written down by the facilitator.

Reflection through discussion of these proverbs, poems and songs will reveal much. What do they mean and what do they imply? who are they intended and in what contexts do they not apply? How true are they? Many are gendered, women and men often having different sayings or different interpretations of sayings. One key element of such proverbs is that they are 'community-binders' – that is, they are common to members of the community and they help to give members of that community a sense of unity. They are often imparted inter-generationally: from grandparents to grandchildren is a frequent route of transmission. Above all, they belong to the community – and thus to the learners. Whereas the textbook (primer) belongs to the government or agency who provides it, proverbs and poems belong to the people. The learners in our programmes will be all the keener to learn to write and then to read these. Indeed, they can be encouraged to generate their own sayings and perhaps write them on the walls of their own houses: there is no need for all writing to be in the learners' exercise book. That will be **building on** these sayings to learn new skills, new knowledge and new attitudes.

Here again the process of CRB (Collecting, Reflecting and Building on) can be most effective. Discovering what proverbs exist in the community, what poems and songs are being used; discussing them in depth to see how they work in the community, to whom they belong; and developing from them new ways for the learners to write, to read and to calculate on paper – these are the ways in which ethnographic approaches to adult literacy and numeracy learning can contribute to make our programmes more effective.

Conclusion

The LETTER participants left the learning programme at this point. All of the participants agreed to take their own studies further by reading; some wanted to do more case studies. All agreed they would try to disseminate the findings of the training programme further – this book is one of the agreed ways of doing this, for the participants intend to use it to train others in this approach. And all agreed they would try to find ways of using ethnographic approaches in the adult literacy learning programmes with which they had contact – either within existing curricula or by developing new curricula.

But we agreed that ethnographic approaches should be regarded as one extra element in such a programme. It has its own limitations. To focus exclusively on the existing literacy and numeracy practices to be found in the communities from which the adult learners come will confine their learning to what is current without introducing them to anything new. To learn about existing uses of calendars, ways of counting and measuring, processes of calculating profit and the range of existing proverbs and sayings without introducing new ways of engaging with all these activities would be to deny the learners the possibility of widening their horizons and adding to the range of options before them. There is much to be learned from critically reflecting on existing practices but there is also much to be learned from other ways of living. The old and the new need to be brought together.

However, what we felt was that it would be advantageous to start with the existing practices and to build on these – not to start with the new and ignore the old. And ethnographic approaches are the best way of identifying the experience, the perceptions, the funds of knowledge and skills, the existing literacy and numeracy practices which the learners bring to the learning programme. That is what this book and the training programme on which it is built are all about.

Some of the participants decided to launch a pilot project of training facilitators in the use of ethnographic approaches to adult literacy and numeracy – forming teams to investigate the existing literacy and numeracy practices in their area and developing new ways of learning literacy and numeracy skills through the themes thrown up by such investigations. Some decided to try to introduce such methods and approaches into their existing teaching and learning programmes. All said they had learned much – not just from the resource persons who helped with the programmes or from each other, but from those they met in the field: the woman who painted pictures and proverbs on the walls of her house, the beggar who lent money to others and the woman who won her suit in court, the seller of cheese, the butcher/house builder, the two women buying and selling bananas secretly to earn some money their husbands cannot reach, the grain seller who used maize seeds to count her money, the weaver and the farmer, the small-scale shop keeper outside the college gates, the farmer's wife who is treasurer of her savings group - these and many others are the people who taught us all so much.

For that is what ethnography does – it turns the world upside down. It teaches the teacher to learn from the learner. And paradoxically in that way we shall create better teaching and learning programmes for everybody.

References and further reading

Barton D, Hamilton M and Ivanic R (eds) *Situated Literacies: reading and writing in context* London: Routledge

Baynham Mike 1995 *Literacy Practices: investigating literacy in social contexts* New York: Longman

Fowler E and Mace J (eds) 2005 *Outside the Classroom: researching literacy with adult learners* Leicester: NIACE

Larson J and Marsh J 2005 *Making Literacy Real: theories and practices for learning and teaching* London: Sage

Mahiri Jabari (ed) 2004 *What Kids Don't Learn in School: literacies for urban youth* New York: P Lang

McCaffrey J, Merrifield J and Millican J 2007 *Developing Adult Literacy: approaches to planning, implementing and delivering literacy initiatives* Oxford: OXFAM

Nirantar 2007 *Exploring the Everyday* New Delhi: Nirantar and ASPBAE

Pahl K and Rowsell J 2005 *Literacy and Education: understanding the New Literacy Studies in the classroom* London: Paul Chapman

Papen Uta 2005 *Adult Literacy as Social Practice: more than skills* London: Routledge

Prinsloo M and Breier M (eds) 1997 *Social Uses of Literacy* Amsterdam: Benjamin, and Johannesburg: SACCHED

Street Brian V (ed) 1995 *Cross-Cultural Approaches to Literacy* Cambridge: Cambridge University Press

Street Brian V (ed) 2001 *Literacy and Development* London: Routledge

Index

Adult Literacy/education/learning 1, 5, 19, 61, 125: and numeracy 2, 9, 125; learning programme - s of 2, 11, 15, 18, 35, 118, 119, 122, 129, 132-134, 148, 150

Agriculture as a main source of income (Ethiopia) 113

Amhura Development Association (ADA) 112

Community Literacy Learning Programmes 18, 35, 118: developing of 18-19

Domestic Literacy Programmes (Ethiopia) 120

ethnographers 6-11, 17, 23, 29, 33

Ethnographic:
adopting in - perspective; adopting - tools 13, 14; conducting - style research 19; conducting research through an - perspective 6, 21, 123; consolidation of - study 33; distinction between approaches carrying out - work 13; examples of developing learning programmes from - findings 145-151; major components of - research 26; methods used for - study 22-24, 38; presentation of - data 8, 31-34; reasons for using - to carry out research 15; tools used to carry out - study/research 23-26, 28; value of - approaches 19, 29

Ethnography 5-7, 9, 10, 12, 13, 15, 19, 126, 151: as a window on literacy and numeracy 15-19; characteristics of 7-13; conducting of 13; definition of 5-6; reasons for using - 9-10; studies of 17, 118, 132-133

Extension workers 1, 2, 113, 134 Agricultural - 134; health - 113, 130, 134

Formal learning/literacy/learning conscious 3, 4, 18, 58, 111, 120, 124, 125, 133

Frierean Literacy 18

Functional Adult Literacy (FAL) Programme 112, 113, 116, 119, 127: and its contribution towards fighting poverty (Ethiopia) 115, 127

Functional Literacy Programme 23

Illiterate(s) (illiteracy) 2, 9-11, 39, 49, 119, 121, 130, 133: bringing of experience and knowledge to learning programmes by 2, 125, 142

Informal learning /informal literacy and tacit fund of knowledge 3-5, 11; building of funds of cultural knowledge through funds of knowledge and practices 4, 5, 14, 15; learning a language as 4; unconscious learning as 4, 5, 123

Land distribution programme (Ethiopia) 113

Land tax (Ethiopia) 107-109

Literacy 1, 4, 5, 15, 17-19, 27: identifying different practices of 16-19; intergrations numeracy with - 122; learner(s) of 11, 14, 124; public - practices 17; schooled 124; skills of 119, 128; uses of 139

153

Literacy and numeracy 1, 4, 5, 15, 17, 19, 20, 22, 25, 27, 28, 34, 54, 118, 126, 133, 135-137, 155: activities of 119; as used in co-operative business 41; as used in small-scale business 50, 52, 53, 83, 127; as used in small scale industry (crafts) 54; events of 17, 111; in context of life histories 86; in market place 59; in rural lives; of farmers 111, 121

Literacy in community 10, 11, 21, 27, 54, 124: uses of 139

Literacy instructors/adult educators 1, 15, 16, 18, 125, 132, 133-136

Literacy - led savings and credit programme 83, 139

Literate(s) 2, 10, 11, 16, 121

Local literacy and numeracy practices 11, 14, 15, 16, 18, 19, 25, 28, 38, 39, 49, 58, 61, 86, 112, 116, 121, 122, 123, 125, 127, 132: features of 121; ethnographic studies about 118; in Ethiopia 39

Micro-credit Scheme (Ethiopia) 39, 40, 44

Non-governmental organisations (WHOs) 132

Religious literacy practices 120, 124

Traditional money lenders (Ethiopia) 67-68

Women (Ethiopia) as members of a micro-credit scheme 40; attitudes of- towards the benefits of microfinance 11, 49, 51; empowerment of illiterate - 9, 39, 89, 129; managing of micro-enterprises by 39, 49, 50, 59, 83

www.ingramcontent.com/pod-product-compliance
Lightning Source LLC
Chambersburg PA
CBHW020617300426
44113CB00007B/676